I Remember Woody

Recollections of the Man
They Called Coach Hayes

Steve Greenberg
and
Dale Ratermann

TRIUMPH
BOOKS
CHICAGO

Library of Congress Cataloging-in-Publication Data

Greenberg, Steve.
    I remember Woody : recollections of the man they called Coach Hayes / Steve Greenberg and Dale Ratermann.
        p. cm.
    Includes index.
    ISBN 1-57243-674-3
        1. Hayes, Woody, 1913–1987. 2. Football coaches—United States—Biography. 3. Ohio State Buckeyes (Football team)—History.   I. Ratermann, Dale, 1956–   II. Title.

GV939.H35G74 2004
796.332'092—dc22
[B]

                                                            2004047853

This book is available in quantity at special discounts for your group or organization. For further information, contact:

Triumph Books
601 South LaSalle Street
Suite 500
Chicago, Illinois 60605
(312) 939-3330
Fax (312) 663-3557

Printed in U.S.A.
ISBN 1-57243-674-3
Design by Patricia Frey

For Dad, who first took me to "The Shoe" in 1961, and for Mom, who "let" us go year after year. My love and gratitude for helping me make this dream come true.
—S.G.

For Emily, Nick, Scott, and Eric.
—D.R.

Contents

Foreword

Woody Hayes. Many people loved him, many hated him, and many didn't understand him. But of all the coaches who I have been fortunate to coach with, or against, he was the greatest.

That's because no coach ever worked harder than Woody. No coach ever had more passion for the game or his players than Woody. And no coach was more committed to win than he was. He was a brilliant teacher and was well-read. He was amazingly honest. And he was loved by almost all of his players. He was, without a doubt, the best ever at teaching the fundamentals of blocking and tackling.

I was lucky to have played for him at Miami (Ohio) University and later coached with him at Ohio State University in 1951 and from 1958 to 1962. A few years afterward, when I got to the University of Michigan in 1969, our teams would meet for the next 10 seasons in late November—and it was usually a gridiron war, with the Big Ten Conference title, a Rose Bowl offer, and a possible national championship often on the line.

He was a friend, a mentor, and a rival.

He had a unique competitiveness about him.

When I was an assistant for him in Columbus, we often had heated debates. Nothing personal, just football techniques or strategy. And he always had the last word.

I probably got fired by Woody at least a dozen times. And was rehired each time—usually 30 minutes later, after he cooled down.

Woody Hayes is memorialized in this homecoming parade float in 1987, seven months after he died. Photo courtesy of Chance Brockway.

But once, it got a lot more heated than usual. We were in a classroom. And to this day, I don't remember what we were arguing about—but I probably didn't agree with his suggestion on how to execute a block.

Well, this time we got carried away. And we got pretty loud, screaming at one another. And before I knew it, he picked up a chair and threw it at me. And I tossed one back at him. We probably tossed a few more back and forth.

Then he got really mad and exploded: *"Schembechler, you're fired!"*

I flew out of the room and headed down the hallway. I eventually went to the locker room to take a shower. Then a minute later, in came Woody. I don't think he followed me, but he must have realized I was in there, too. As he headed out the door I heard him say, "I'll see you in the morning, Bo." Just like that, I was forgiven.

Many times I'd get a telephone call from him early in the morning or after I'd gone home. After picking up the receiver, Woody would be barking: *"Meet me at the racquetball court in half an hour, Bo. If you're not there, it's because you can't take it."*

And I'd always show up and we'd go at it for an hour or so. He loved to try to wear me out on the racquetball court.

Woody was a complex person. Talented, hard-driving, but very caring. Most of America knows him for his great winning teams and his sideline tantrums. But hundreds of people in Columbus know him for the times he'd stop by the hospital, or by someone's house, to visit with someone who was sick—people he didn't even know but had heard about. But that was Woody—a guy with a big heart.

Once, when I was a senior playing for Woody at Miami, our team was flying back to Ohio after playing Arizona State University in the Salad Bowl, which we won. On our trip home, we had to make an unscheduled stop in Nashville to sit out a thunderstorm. It was after midnight. And we were hungry.

After we got in the airport lobby, Woody went to see the manager of the restaurant that overlooked the airfield. He was getting ready to close.

Woody explained, "We've got to get these guys something to eat."

The guy looked over at out team. Then he pointed to Boxcar Bailey, a great fullback who ran the 100-yard dash in 9.5 seconds, and the only black ballplayer on our team.

"That guy isn't going to eat here," he said.

Woody just stared at him. "What do you mean, he isn't?"

"We don't serve his kind," the restaurant manager said.

"If that guy doesn't eat here, then none of us will eat here," Woody shot back.

A bit embarrassed, the restaurant manager stammered, "Well, he can't eat right here, but perhaps he can eat upstairs."

Feeling pleased at the headway he was making, Woody remarked, "Fine. Then we'll all eat upstairs."

"There's not enough room for everybody up there," the man explained.

Wayne Woodrow Hayes: 1913–1987. Photo courtesy of Ohio State University Sports Information Department.

Bo Schembechler (left) shares an uncharacteristic light moment with Woody Hayes before an Ohio State–Michigan game. Schembechler was Hayes' most bitter rival on the field and his closest friend off it. Photo courtesy of Chance Brockway.

Wearing a stare that I will always remember, Woody told the guy, "Then Boxcar and I will eat upstairs together and the rest of the team will eat downstairs."

Woody won us all over that night.

Just like he would win over his other teams with memorable examples of leadership and character. And that's why his teams had such great success.

The day before he passed away, he traveled nearly 75 miles, from Columbus to Dayton, to introduce me at a luncheon.

By this point, Woody had grown frail after a stroke and was sitting in a wheelchair. But he wanted to brag about one of his boys.

He charmed us all that day.

Woody was indeed a very special man. A teacher who taught many of us some important lessons in life that will be long remembered.

I miss him a lot.

—Bo Schembechler
Former head coach, University of Michigan

Acknowledgments

We offer our sincere thanks on several fronts to many folks, without whose help the writing of this book would have been much more difficult. Mitch Rogatz, Tom Bast, and Blythe Hurley of Triumph Books believed in the project from the beginning, and for that we are grateful. The people we interviewed—all of them—enthusiastically and unselfishly gave us a great deal of their time. Perhaps most instrumental in getting this project off the ground was Steve Snapp, the sports information director at Ohio State. He provided us with countless contacts and ideas.

Others who did heavy lifting on our behalf deserve salutes, most notably former OSU standouts Larry Zelina, Rex Kern, Tom Skladany, Neal Colzie (may he rest in peace), William B. Hoyer, and the many secretaries, administrative assistants, and sports information personnel we pestered across the country.

Rick Van Brimmer, the director of licensing at OSU, and Jim Sims, Steve Parker, and Eric Whitcher of Kingston got this baby licensed, and we certainly appreciate and value their expertise. Jim Lachey, the radio analyst for OSU football and a former NFL and OSU star, and Jon Self and the staff at the Buckeye Hall of Fame Café, continue to be more than gracious in support. R. J. Cavallero, who is going to get this on a screen somewhere, is a big believer, and we appreciate that.

On a personal note, I'd like to thank Roscoe for the longstanding partnership, Sparky and the staff of the s/v *Fly Hoopdee* for the lovely cruise, Teri ("Chuck") Norris, who kept the coffee coming at corporate, Mr. Mon for the coaching, and Moon, Dr. Williams, Hondo, and Bubba for the music. Last, but certainly not least (great cliché), let's have a round of applause for my bride, Sally, and daughters Annie and Rachel for their love and support, which helped to fuel this mission. All y'all done good!

—Steve Greenberg
Carmel, Indiana

—Dale Ratermann
Indianapolis, Indiana

*"I will be proud to lead you wonderful guys
into battle anytime, anywhere."*

—U.S. Army General George S. Patton,
one of Woody Hayes' military heroes

Briefing

Woody Hayes was one of the most colorful characters college football has ever known. It's doubtful there will ever be another like him.

These days, a good many coaches are more chairmen of the boards than they are real people. The real people rant and rave; they make mistakes; they deeply care about whether their charges graduate and make lives for themselves after football. They wear their emotions proudly, and they don't give a damn what people think about them.

Hayes put it like this to a documentary film crew from England in 1977: "You know, the older I get—and I shouldn't say this because it'll always be misconstrued—but the older I get, the less I care about what they say. I'm sorry. I have to level with Woody Hayes, but I don't have to level with them. As long as I feel I'm treating these youngsters right and I'm trying honestly to help them get an education, I don't care much what they say."

No, Woody Hayes was no board guy. He was a legend, a giant of the game, a true warrior in his own cantankerous, crafty, and crusty way. He was a tactician, he refused to be outworked, he challenged his players to give their best efforts, and he never backed down from a challenge.

"Coaching is a lot of fun because it's so enormously competitive," Hayes said to an interviewer from WBNS-TV in Columbus, Ohio, in the mid-eighties. "And to win, you've got to get these other people competitive and playing on a team . . . and that's the fun of the whole thing."

He was impassioned by his varied interests, among them football, military history, civil rights, and literature. How many coaches stopped practice to recite the writings of Ralph Waldo Emerson or Chairman Mao, or cite the virtues of General George S. Patton or other military icons? Only Woody.

Intellectual and committed to education though he was, mostly he was a coach, although "it was not exactly a goal of mine. I never thought I'd get that far." But it turned out to be his life.

When Hayes was inducted into the National Football Foundation Hall of Fame on December 9, 1983, he tried, in his own rambling yet forceful way, to explain football's place in his life.

Said Hayes, jaw firmly clenched and his trademark lisp punctuating his oratory: "You know, people say to me, 'What do you get out of football?' So, I'd invariably ask my players, 'What do you get out of football?' . . . 'What do you get? Well, number one is, Coach, when you get knocked down you learn to get up and go once more.'

"And then the other thing that becomes so important in football is the fact that nothing in this world that comes easy is worth a dime. Nothing that comes easy is worth anything. I've never yet seen a football player make a tackle with a smile on his face."

But there was so much more to Woody Hayes than most realize. In an age when so many people preached about paying back, Woody Hayes was drilling his players about paying forward. Take care of the future, he'd tell them. As a prime example of how his teachings time and again have been heeded, several members of the 1968 Ohio State University national championship team gathered in 1988 for homecoming at Columbus and presented the university with more than $1 million. A lesson learned.

Hayes died on March 12, 1987. In the months leading up to his death at age 74, he was a mere shadow of what he used to be. Oh, he was still feisty at times. But mostly he was frail, dependent on his cane, and in ill health. Diabetes, high blood pressure, and heart disease had caught up with him.

He may be gone, but the mere mention of his name brings an anecdote here, or a full-blown story there, and, almost always, a smile or a frown. Many times, the recollection will be of the incident that proved most costly of all to the coach, the one about how he slugged Clemson University middle guard Charlie Bauman after Bauman intercepted Ohio State quarterback Art Schlichter's pass

Team meetings, regardless of whether they were conducted in the locker room or at the training facility, were serious business to Woody Hayes. Photo courtesy of Ohio State University Sports Information Department.

late in the nationally televised 1978 Gator Bowl at Jacksonville, Florida. Hayes was fired the next morning.

Add it up: 28 seasons of coaching the Buckeyes; a 205–61–10 OSU record, including 152 conference wins; only 2 losing seasons; 4 consecutive Rose Bowl appearances (the only coach to achieve that); 11 total bowl appearances, including 8 Rose Bowls; 56 players selected as All-Americans; 13 Big Ten Conference championships; 17 consecutive Big Ten victories (achieved twice); 5 national titles; 3 Heisman Trophy winners; 3 Outland Trophy winners; 2 Lombardi Award winners; 2 national coach-of-the-year awards; and 1 deadly quiet last charter flight back to Port Columbus International Airport.

Three weeks after his firing, as he was addressing a Columbus Chamber of Commerce luncheon, he all but apologized for his actions at the Gator Bowl.

"I feel very, very sorry for it because of all the wonderful people it's affected—my coaches, who are without jobs. We've got to help them get a job. . . . We've got to do that."

And years later in an interview with WBNS, this: "I made a lot of mistakes. When you do a lot of things, you're bound to make mistakes. And you get tired and make mistakes, too. Defeat is a great cleanser, and it's what you do from there that really counts. And you find so many times that person or that team or that nation is totally defeated. Well, they come back. And if you don't believe me, watch out or you'll get run over by a Toyota or a Mercedes."

In the autumn of his life, Hayes was honored in countless ways. In 1982, Ohio State renamed University Drive as Woody Hayes Drive during a public ceremony; an east–west road, it runs past the north end of Ohio Stadium. In 1983, he was accorded the honor every true Buckeye wishes for: dotting the *i* in the Ohio State marching band's incomparable Script Ohio formation. And in 1986, he was given the Amos Alonzo Stagg Award for meritorious service to the coaching profession. As recently as the spring of 1997, bronze busts of Hayes— complete with his baseball hat—were being sold for $5,000 each to help raise money for an academic scholarship in his memory at the university.

To suggest, as some have, that Woody Hayes boiled down to a one-punch firing would be terribly incorrect. It's not that simple, and he was not a simple man.

Hayes was one of impeccable moral fiber, a giant of a man who, when addressing commencement participants at OSU a few months before his death, said haltingly with tears streaming down his face, "This is the greatest day of my life." And then, as one might expect, he used the forum to launch into an address that included, among other topics, paying forward and shaping the future. It didn't sound like the person who had spent countless hours, deep into the night, breaking down game or practice film on a rickety old projector—possibly the same kind of projector he smashed to the floor in anger during a meeting with his coaching staff many years before.

Bo Schembechler, Hayes' most bitter rival on the field for 10 seasons and one of his closest friends off the field, talks about Woody in *Bo* (Warner Books, 1989):

". . . He made mistakes. His temper was, at times, inexcusable. But he shaped me and everything I do with a stamp of passion and strength. He was a remarkable coach, a teacher, a winner. I will miss him forever, and I'll never meet another man like him. Not in this world, anyway."

Schembechler, who wrote the foreword for this book, isn't the only one who misses Hayes. Many folks long for the days when there was a rotund man in white shirtsleeves stomping his way up and down the Ohio Stadium sideline, barking out instructions, admonishing referees, cheering his players, slapping his players, holding his audiences completely spellbound, jostling with the media, and being convinced that the other guys were spying on him.

Steve Hayes, Woody and Anne's only child, once characterized his father as a man who was volatile, had a temper, and had a drive that never quit. "His temper was built into his drive," Steve said to a WBNS interviewer in the mid-eighties. "I don't think you could separate one from the other." Steve, now a judge in Columbus, said he experienced more than his fair share of the gentle, caring, and giving side of his dad, but Anne and Woody in tandem constituted a nearly immovable force. "We were not a laid-back household," he said. "When they were together, they were a lot of trouble."

Not a single thing about Woody Hayes was half-baked. As a husband and father—and grandfather to Phillip and Laura Hayes—he loved and he was loved. As a coach, he educated. As an educator, he coached. He was the embodiment of the old saying about success coming when preparation meets opportunity. This was a man who

A smiling Woody Hayes marches off the Ohio Stadium field in 1983 after living every true Buckeye's dream: dotting the i in the marching band's incomparable Script Ohio formation. Photo courtesy of Chance Brockway.

pulled all the niggling details together and almost always made Christmas morning—Game Day—just right for Buckeyes fans everywhere.

There was a time when, as soon as summer came, he would take trips to the front lines in Vietnam to cheer the U.S. troops and show them football films. Then he'd return stateside and call or write the family of every serviceman with whom he visited—all at his own expense.

Understand, money meant very little to Hayes. He often refused to cash checks given to him after speaking engagements and just as often gave those same types of checks to persons in need. He refused salary increases. He refused contract increases for his television show.

He visited an untold number of patients in hospitals in Columbus and across the country. He just wanted to encourage them, to cheer them, to let them know someone cared. He even knew some of them.

Ohio State played the game long before Hayes ever heard of the university, but he was the one to attach the label of superiority to its program and the one who led its followers to bleed scarlet and gray. Woody Hayes lived his occupation, took care of his players, and had an unrelenting hunger for victory.

A legend? Yes. A tradition? Absolutely, to this day.

* * *

Born on February 14, 1913, in Clifton, Ohio, Wayne Woodrow Hayes led an active childhood, to say the least.

He and his brother, Isaac, two years his senior, often would engage in boxing . . . many times with each other. It would become a problem for his parents, Wayne B. and Effie Jane Hupp Hayes, and his sister, Mary, who was eight years older. Those Hayes boys were tough guys and enforcers, and they were successful at almost every endeavor.

Clyde Barthalow, one of his teachers, told a WBNS film crew that Hayes was a gifted athlete "and always at the center of every activity. He also was a voracious reader who enjoyed the battles of the great wars. He was one of the most interesting students I ever had."

Perhaps taking a cue from his father, a school superintendent, Hayes immersed himself in academics at an early age. Sports were important to him, to be sure, but nothing could take the place of his cherished collection of books. Hayes developed a discipline with books early on, so much so, in fact, that he pursued education with a hunger that usually only the best and brightest pupils exhibit. A good student, he was determined not to be outworked, a characteristic that stayed with him until his dying day.

Said Barthalow: "Woody extended himself because he wanted to meet his father's approval as far as his education was concerned. If there's such a thing as immortality, it's carried on by Woody from his father."

Still, sports held a place in his heart. Everyone knows him for football, but at Newcomerstown (Ohio) High School, basketball became his first love. He got by on the court not on athletic aptitude but on toughness and perseverance. Better at football, Hayes was captain of the Newcomerstown team, but he still was not all-star caliber.

He also played baseball, and it was the legendary Cy Young who held young Hayes' attention. Young, a baseball immortal and Hall of Famer, was a native of Newcomerstown, a fact not lost on Hayes. In the days after his retirement from the pro game, Young would play host to beer bashes at his farm, and to keep things lively he'd stage boxing matches in his barn. The bouts featured youngsters from the community, many of them content to walk away with a sawbuck for their efforts. Among them? If you guessed Woody Hayes, go to the head of the class.

The head of the class is where Hayes wanted to be. After graduating from high school in 1931, he decided to enroll at Denison University in Granville, Ohio, where he pursued a double major in English and history. Apparently content to drop his fists and hit the books, he went after academics as a shark would a flailing fish. He developed a reputation as a top-notch student. So proficient and confident was Hayes that he decided to look into the possibility of law school.

But then the Great Depression took hold. In dire need of money, he jumped tracks and set off on a career as an educator. But a funny thing happened on the way to the class-room and that $1,200 annual salary at Mingo Junction (Ohio) High School. The position also required him to be an assistant football coach. Fate?

To this day, many football fans bless the day the English-teaching and football-coaching jobs were tied to one full-time position. And to this day, many curse that same day.

Hayes left Mingo Junction after one year, and before settling in the autumn at New Philadelphia (Ohio) High School—where he taught history and also was an assistant football coach—he enrolled in graduate school at

A happy moment during an eighties celebration of his coaching career. Photo courtesy of Ohio State University Sports Information Department.

Ohio State. If he couldn't be a lawyer, he would be in education administration as was his father. Several summers of part-time graduate courses later, the master's degree was his.

During his quest for the master's, Hayes began what amounted to a four-year courtship with, and later a lifelong commitment to, Anne Gross of New Philadelphia. They were married on June 19, 1942, while the enlisted sailor Hayes was rising to the rank of destroyer escort commander in the Pacific Ocean. "That was supposed to be Emancipation Day," Anne Hayes would say later, adding jokingly, "I was sold into slavery." Discharged in 1946, Hayes carried with him for the rest of his life a deep love for his Annie and a deep passion for military history.

His first head coaching job was at New Philadelphia in 1938. The first season, his team finished 9–1. The second season, it was 9–0–1. Then the bottom fell out; with too many graduating seniors to replace, Hayes' third New Philadelphia team finished 1–9. About seven months later, he was off to officers' training school in the U.S. Navy.

Coming home from the Pacific, Hayes applied for and was granted the opportunity to revive the dormant football program at Denison. He took almost anyone who wanted to play, including beer-swilling ex-seamen. His first season ended 2–9. Then the lava in Hayes spewed over the rim. With physical fitness and a no-nonsense approach at the center of his Big Red program, Hayes led Denison to a 9–0 record in 1947 and 8–0 in 1948.

It wasn't lost on the folks in Oxford, Ohio, home of Miami University. They brought Hayes in to lead the Redskins football program. And by the second season, 1950, they more than received their money's worth; Miami finished the regular season 8–1, whipped bitter rival University of Cincinnati, 28–0, in the regular-season finale, and went on to defeat Arizona State University in the Salad Bowl.

Just a couple months later, a university on the banks of the Olentangy River in Columbus, Ohio, came calling in search of a head football coach to replace the departed Wes Fesler.

Sixty-one years and 19 coaching appointments after founding its football program in 1890, Ohio State had its man, and his name was Wayne Woodrow Hayes.

Woody Hayes has not been forgotten. Often misunderstood and controversial, the former coach is remembered in the following pages by those who knew him best: his players, his staff, his adversaries, his friends, and his fans.

Chapter One

The Players

Ken Fritz, Brian Baschnagel, Archie Griffin, Larry Zelina, Rex Kern, Calvin Murray, Frank "Moose" Machinsky, Paul Warfield, Chuck Hutchison, Steve Luke, Steve Myers, Neal Colzie, Ted Provost, Ron Ayers, Tom DeLeone, Doug Plank, Greg Lashutka, Tom Marendt, John Hicks, Randy Hart, Carm Cozza, Don Sutherin, Jimmy Moore, Randy Gradishar, Dean Dugger

"…Guys like Bo Schembechler, Woody Hayes, and Bear Bryant were all helped by their dominating personalities, but they were helped even more by superb players."

—Doug Looney, *Sports Illustrated*

As Ohio State was driving for the lead, and possibly the victory, in the 1978 Gator Bowl, Art Schlichter's pass was intercepted by Clemson University middle guard Charlie Bauman. Bauman ran along the Ohio State sideline with the ball in one hand, seemingly taunting coach Woody Hayes and the rest of the Ohio State team.

Ken Fritz was an offensive guard on that Buckeyes team, and he was an up-close witness to the end of an era. "A very touching moment" is how Fritz describes it during what he acknowledges is the only interview he has granted on the subject.

"Charlie Bauman definitely taunted us," says Fritz, now married and the father of two boys in Columbus, where he is an insurance executive. And in retaliation, Hayes slugged Bauman. Fritz recalls it clearly. "Woody hit him and then I put a bear hug on Woody. He kept yelling, 'Let me go! Let me go!' Many people believe Woody actually hit me [it appears to be the case in photos of the scene], but he really was just pushing my face mask away. If I had let him go, he would have gotten back into the middle of the scuffle.

"Man. He was the most intense human being on the face of the earth."

Fritz sees the Gator Bowl incident, which he says clearly was ignited by Bauman "making comments and gestures at us," as a horrendously sour experience.

"First of all, the Gator Bowl was intended for an [Atlantic Coast Conference] team to beat up on another school. It was a tense, miserable, bitter week," Fritz says. "Clemson got fifty thousand tickets, I think, and we got five thousand. It was the worst bowl game I ever played in."

When it all boiled to the surface and Hayes had thrown his punch, the game clearly was lost, and the team was lost in its thoughts and emotions, Fritz says.

"When the game was over, Woody never said a word," Fritz says. "We all got dressed and went to the buses. He still didn't say anything. The next morning, as we were preparing to leave Jacksonville for Columbus, he said nothing. On the flight home, he sat in the back of the plane, saying nothing. When we got to the Columbus airport, they had two undercover officers there, who took him down the back steps of the plane, put him in their car, and drove him home. They never put him in the public eye. I thought they did a fabulous job."

Fritz sums up the incident this way: "It made Woody look like an animal, and he wasn't! Hey, you and I would've done the same thing. Woody Hayes did not want to hurt Charlie Bauman.

"You know, Charlie called Woody a couple days later and they discussed what happened. And Woody told him, 'You're a young man. We all make mistakes. I'm an older man and nobody cares.' Woody Hayes ended up protecting Charlie Bauman! And Charlie found respect for him."

Fritz says he believes he would not have been able to attain the success he enjoys today, inside and outside the business world, had it not been for Hayes. "He was the hardest worker anywhere," Fritz says. "And he was always on you to make the best out of yourself, especially in school. He gave you every opportunity to be successful.

"Woody Hayes, to me, was my protector, my father, my mother, my minister all in one. He just kind of had that power. It's still amazing what that 'extra' power helps me do."

For example, Fritz says he rises between 5:30 and 6:00 A.M. daily and goes to work out—this from a man who walked away from the game he dearly loved after he was exposed to its underbelly as a member of the Pittsburgh Steelers in 1981. "I just quit," he says. "Couldn't stand the politics."

Those early morning workouts, though, at the time of day during which Hayes would accomplish a great deal, Fritz says, are the foundation for his day. He says Hayes once told a World War II story about how a group of German soldiers was caught with its guard down. "Woody said it was early in the morning, and they were fat, drunk, and some were asleep. [The allies] ambushed 'em. It pays to get a head start.

"It does work! Like Woody, I believe I can get a lot more accomplished between 8:00 and 1:00 than most people can who start at 10:00. I get a two-hour head start on them and don't look back. It's discipline, and that's what Woody stood for."

The Old Coach also stood for education in a big way. "Many never got to see how Woody was about education, but he stayed on us all the time," Fritz says. "From what I understand, when I was playing for Ohio State he was graduating 88 percent of his players; there might've been only one or two schools ahead of him. That's pretty impressive, don't you think?"

Fritz remembers, too, the fits Hayes used to throw.

"He'd be punching himself in the jaw. He'd cuss himself. He'd feel that he was letting us down if something didn't go right," Fritz recalls. "He was such a perfectionist. You'd listen to him, but you thought he was crazy at times. But then I was just a typical kid back then. When I was about 30 years old and I had kids, though, it really hit me that I was acting like Woody around them."

Fritz says that's a good thing. It goes back to his deep respect for his mentor. And that respect led him into Hayes' office one day during his sophomore season.

"I was going to get married before my junior year, and Woody asked me to bring my [fiancée] in with me for an interview," Fritz recalls with a laugh. "Woody just had to approve her. He had to make you aware that maybe it's something you shouldn't do.

"So he started to interview her, with me sitting there, and he asked her what her intentions were, and he let her know about the demands on me as a football player and student.

"He came to find out we had common interests, and he approved. But this lecturing and counseling and interviewing went on for one-and-a-half to two hours before he said OK."

Fritz says he "could sit and talk with Woody for hours and hours and football would never come up. He always had something good to tell you. In that way, he was like a father. I still have his picture on my desk and one on the wall in my family room. It'll always remain there."

Work ethic. Discipline. Intensity. Fritz rattles off the attributes of his former coach.

"He'd be like [sometimes-embattled former Indiana University basketball coach] Bobby Knight is today. That's good," Fritz says. "Let me tell you, I'd send my kid to play for Bobby Knight in a heartbeat. I would love for my son to play for him. He's just like Woody."

Remember Woody Hayes, Fritz implores, not for the Gator Bowl incident but for all the good he did when he was alive.

"He helped and shaped so many people, it's unbelievable. I'd venture to guess that he has as many or more former players who are millionaires—outside of football—than any coach in the country, and that's because he was good to them, he showed them the way, he encouraged them, he helped them, and he loved them."

* * *

Fortuitous. That's what first comes to mind when Brian Baschnagel is asked about Woody Hayes.

"His foresight was incredible, just incredible," says Baschnagel, who from 1972 to 1975 was a wingback for the Buckeyes and who was an Academic All-America and Academic All–Big Ten choice as well as a National Football Foundation Hall of Fame Scholarship winner in 1975.

"Woody said I'd play 10 years in the NFL, which is exactly what happened," says the former wide receiver for the Chicago Bears.

To fully appreciate the measure of Hayes' ability to predict, listen to Baschnagel: "I went to high school in Pittsburgh—we had moved 16 times since I was born [in Kingston, New York]—and our team had some success my junior and senior years. Four of us altogether were offered scholarships, a couple partial. We were going to go to the same school.

"I am Catholic. We moved a lot, but the one team I really could identify with was Notre Dame. I was a big Domer. I was recruited by Notre Dame, Penn State, Michigan, Ohio State, and some other Big Ten schools.

"I didn't want to go to Ohio State. I was an O. J. Simpson fan and had watched Ohio State beat USC in the [January 1, 1969] Rose Bowl. I just didn't want to [visit] there, although there was no reason not to go. . . .

"Woody, as he always was, was quite involved in recruiting. He did a lot of personal visits [to prospects' homes and schools]. He called me

Brian Baschnagel (No. 48), Archie Griffin (No. 45), and Tim Fox (No. 12) await the coin toss at midfield. Photo courtesy of Ohio State University Sports Information Department.

and said, 'Brian, I'd like to take you out to dinner.' This was prior to my visit in 1972. He came out to Pittsburgh, and I said to him, 'Coach, I have volleyball practice.' He said, 'No problem. I'll come to the school. I'll wait for you.'

"I was very nervous, but all my buddies were really excited; they thought they had a chance to show coach Hayes their talents. He was a renowned coach. Anyway, whenever I did something good at practice, I looked over to where coach Hayes was sitting. He sat on a bench the whole time and read a book, *Animal Farm*. I don't think he ever looked at me. After practice was over, I took a quick shower and we went out to dinner.

"We were at [the restaurant] for three hours and he never talked about football. We talked about a lot of things, and he asked me about my likes and dislikes, but we never talked about football. He took a very personal interest in me.

"He asked me what academic goals I had. I said I was thinking about business school, although I really didn't know at the time. But he spent several minutes promoting Ohio State's business school. He talked about all the successful businessmen that came out of football and Ohio State. And then I mentioned law school. Same thing.

"I was pretty impressed by it. It was quite unusual. No coach personally ever came out to visit me. I still didn't want to [take the trip to] Ohio State. But a few weeks later I went. I had just an OK time. It was a nice campus, huge, and I kind of liked it. I left Ohio State, and Woody put on some pressure. I didn't care for it, but he needed to do it. He said, 'Would you like to come to Ohio State?' I said, 'Yeah,' even though I hadn't made up my mind. 'OK, we'll sign the papers now.' I told him I had other visits planned to Notre Dame and other schools. He backed off immediately. No pressure. He made no promises. I ended up visiting Notre Dame. I kept thinking that if I went to Ohio State, I had confidence in my abilities and anything could happen. Who knows? I knew I would get my education regardless of what happened.

"I decided I was going to go to Ohio State because of Woody."

As luck would have it, Baschnagel was recruited to play tailback for the Buckeyes. "That's the same position Archie [Griffin] played and, of course, that didn't work out," he says. "So I learned a new position, and it was a tremendous experience for me. I was blocking and catching, although we were a running attack and we all knew it. But going to Ohio State was a tremendous development for me. It's what made me a professional athlete. We ended up going to four Rose Bowls and we had a lot of success."

On National Football League draft day in the spring of 1976, Baschnagel found himself with a heavy load—and not a bit of it was related to where he would be taken in the draft or by which team. "I had an oral presentation, a paper due, one midterm, and one significant quiz," he says as if it were just yesterday. "But I'm walking back . . . and I got to thinking, I wonder if I got drafted. Then I was starting to get a little nervous. Maybe it was the lack of sleep; I was a crammer, and I had been up most of the night. Maybe it was the draft. Maybe it was a combination of the two.

"Gary McCutcheon was my roommate, we were both seniors, and he was back manning the phones in case a team called. If I had been drafted, I knew he would have told me right away. But he didn't say anything. We had some small talk and played some gin.

"Then he said, 'Pittsburgh called and wondered if you were interested in playing for them.' I said, 'What did you tell them?' He said, 'Yeah.'

"A few minutes later, he said, 'Washington called'—and they had no pick until the fifth round—and I said, 'What did you tell them?' And he said, 'Yeah.'

"Then he hands me a beer and says, 'Oh, by the way, congratulations. The Bears drafted you in the third round and you need to call [general manager] Jim Finks right away.'

"Well, my hands were shaking, and we had one of those old dial phones, and I couldn't dial it. I said, 'Gary, you gotta dial this phone for me!' When Jim Finks answers, he says, 'Welcome aboard. What position do you want to play?' And I'm thinking, What is this, a pickup game? Jim says, 'We drafted you as an athlete. What position do you want to play?' . . . I ended up as a wide receiver."

Several weeks after the draft Hayes summoned Baschnagel to his office. Hayes was extremely serious, as was usually the case.

Baschnagel was braced for the questions, but he wondered if he had the correct answers.

"He said to me, 'Brian, what are you going to do?' And I smiled and said, 'Coach, what do you mean what am I going to do?' And he said, 'I mean after you graduate!' And I said, 'Coach, I have been drafted by the Bears.'

"Then he takes a book and slams it down and says, 'There goes your law career!' We ended up having it out. We went back and forth.

"I said, 'You're asking me to deny myself an opportunity to continue my football career? I'll go to Chicago, make the team, and get a law degree.' And he says, 'I know you, Brian. You're going to Chicago, you'll make the team, you'll play 10 years, and you'll never get your law degree!'"

During his first off-season with the Bears, Baschnagel returned to Columbus. It was nice, he says, to have the time off to recover from the contact and other rigors of the professional game. He also saw it as a chance to prepare for the next season.

"I went to see Woody at his office," Baschnagel remembers. "His desk was pointed away from the door. I said, 'Coach?' And he said, 'Come on in.' He never looked at me. After realizing who had entered, he never said anything else. He just pointed to the door.

"I said, 'Coach, I just came by to say hi.' He pointed to the door and said, 'Don't come back until you're enrolled in law school.'"

Almost immediately, Baschnagel rushed down to the registrar's office and enrolled himself for a second major in accounting. "I thought I might become a [certified public accountant], but really my sole purpose for doing that was to get in to see Woody. No way was I going to law school.

"So I go back to his office, and it's the same thing. I said to him, 'Coach, I'm in school!' We started chatting.

"I was telling that story to a reporter in 1987 . . . when it dawned on me that Woody accomplished exactly what he wanted. He was just manipulative enough to prepare me for life after football. It all goes back to that three-hour dinner."

And as you might recall, Baschnagel played almost 10 seasons with the Bears—as Hayes had predicted—before injuries forced him out of the game.

When he looks back at his relationship with Hayes, he sees this: "A great teacher. A concerned citizen. Someone [for] who[m] you could say, 'Everything he did had a purpose.' His convictions were so strong. He fought for everything he believed in," Baschnagel says. "I'm extremely proud to have played for the guy. . . .

"Woody was quite the guy. I miss him. It's not the same going back to Ohio State now. He was such an important figure. I still respect the university, but, to me, Ohio State was Woody Hayes."

* * *

Archie Griffin was Woody Hayes' favorite player of all those he coached. And why not? In Griffin you have the only two-time Heisman Trophy winner in history, a three-time All-American, the only player to amass 100 yards or more in 31 consecutive games, the only player to lead Ohio State in rushing four consecutive seasons, and the only player to start four Rose Bowl games. There are many other records set by Griffin, and many more honors. But to hear the man, who now is the executive director of the Ohio State University Alumni Association, tell it, it all paled in comparison to playing for and learning from Hayes.

"He was such a caring person," Griffin says. "He was always thinking of others. When he'd pull you aside away from football, and sometimes during football, he'd talk to you about life in general."

Griffin says he might have been close to being an also-ran in OSU's stable of thoroughbreds during his freshman season in 1972.

"I was on the scout team for the Iowa game," Griffin recalls. "We were way ahead, and coach Hayes finally put me in. Well, I fumbled that first handoff and came out. Rudy Hubbard, the running back coach, stayed on coach Hayes. He believed in me and wanted coach Hayes to believe, too. He pounded the table for me to go in again.

11

Griffin wends his way through the defense. Photo courtesy of Ohio State University Sports Information Department.

Coach Hayes was convinced, and I started the next game against North Carolina."

The game against the Tar Heels was a coming-out party for one of the most prolific running backs of all time. Griffin got the ball early and often, pounding up the middle, over the top, and skirting off tackles for a then–school record 239 yards. Hayes knew a good thing when he saw one, and thus the legend was launched.

"I'm glad it happened that way," Griffin says of his shaky first game and record-shattering second outing. "If I had known I was going to start and had been with the team at the hotel the night before the game, I might've been a nervous wreck!"

Griffin, to this day, seems to want to pinch himself to see if it's all real. The beginning, way before the fumble against Iowa, was a true test administered by the coach.

"When coach Hayes was recruiting me, I was convinced he didn't want me. The first time we met, we never talked about football. We talked about everything but football. I went home and told my father [the late James Griffin], 'Daddy, I don't know if he wants me to play football.' And my dad said, 'Son, he's concerned with you as a person first.' But Ohio State continued to recruit me, and when I finally got the call, I was told if I was in for anything other than a good education, I might as well leave."

Clearly, Griffin is convinced his decision to go to Ohio State was the best he could have made. In a way, he was following his heart, too.

"Having grown up in Columbus, it was wonderful," Griffin says. "I grew up around Ohio State football. I was kind of in awe about the whole thing, because I seriously didn't think Ohio State would try to recruit me."

More than the football games—which included a run of 40–5–1 through the competition, helping him to eventually be inducted into the National Football Foundation Hall of Fame, the Rose Bowl Hall of Fame, and the Ohio State University Athletic Hall of Fame—Griffin says his personal interaction with Hayes was what made his college career a complete experience.

"Woody Hayes was one who had a tremendous impact on me. He was so caring, and yes, he was a great football coach. But he was very knowledgeable, he was dedicated, and was a true leader. He worked harder than anyone else, and he always seemed to be able to work his way through life's ups and downs. Coach Hayes was a giant among men."

* * *

The Super Sophs were an accomplished bunch, and probably Woody Hayes' greatest recruiting class. You can tick off the names: Stillwagon, Tatum, Kern, White, Brockington, Anderson, Sensibaugh, Jankowski, and last but not least, Zelina—Larry Zelina, the undersized wingback from Cleveland who played for Augie Bossu, the winningest high school coach of all time.

Zelina, now an insurance company executive in Columbus, prefers to think of Woody Hayes not as a football coach but as a human being.

"He was a great humanitarian," says Zelina, who played for OSU from 1968 to 1970. "Woody cared more about us as people rather than football players. He wanted to see us succeed as human beings, and to that end he led by example. People don't know about the many things he did for 'the common person.' That's not good copy. His temper made good copy. But he would do anything he could to help whoever he could, and he would often go out of his way to do it."

Zelina, married and the father of three children, says Hayes was extremely demanding, more so of himself than of his players. And because the coach was able to meet his own demands most of the time, his players followed suit. It's no accident, then, that the Super Sophs roared through three seasons with a 27–2 record and won the 1968 national championship.

Hayes was always teaching and leading, Zelina recalls, adding that he and several of his former teammates draw from those lessons in their everyday and work lives today.

"We all still use a lot of his teachings to this day," Zelina says. "He stood for being fair and honest, not being afraid to get your fingers dirty, to set and achieve goals but do it fairly, and to be true and faithful to yourself and those who are important to you.

"I don't think that a day goes by that I don't think about Woody. He and my high school coach and my dad were the great influences in my life. They all taught me how to live life and treat others around me. I was a pretty lucky guy."

There were times during his days under Hayes that Zelina was left wondering what the heck was going on. But there always seemed to be a method to the madness.

"For example, our trip to the Rose Bowl was a four-hour flight from Columbus," Zelina says. "Woody was real concerned about us being distracted for the January 1, 1969, game. So he used that four-hour flight to help keep us focused. We actually had meetings on the plane. You had the line meeting here, the backs there, the defense in the back of the plane. He refused to let us get caught up in the fanfare that was waiting for us in Los Angeles."

To further underscore his wishes, Hayes actually had the training staff tape the ankles of his California-bound players.

Larry Zelina (No. 16) makes tracks against Purdue during the 13–0 victory in 1968. Photo courtesy of Ohio State University Sports Information Department.

"There we were in jackets and ties getting taped," Zelina recalls, laughing at the memory. "Then he tells us we're going to practice in our sweats as soon as we can after we land. So we get there and they drive us to the Sheraton. The [Rose Bowl] princesses were there, and here we come walking in wearing our shirts, ties, and Ohio State gray sport coats . . . with taped ankles!"

Zelina says for the Rose Bowl following the 1970 season, he and some of the players talked with Hayes about the upcoming flight to the West Coast. "We told him, 'Please, Coach, we don't want to get taped on the plane again.' And he seemed to agree," Zelina says. "Then sometime during the flight Woody says, 'There's too much levity here! Goddamn it! There's too much smiling going on here.' He had them tape us again . . . after he promised he wouldn't."

Preparedness was an obsession with Hayes. "Woody was a great coach, a great motivator, and a great teacher. He really taught us lessons," Zelina says. "What he lacked in imagination, he made up for with hard work."

And that hard work spilled over into offseason recruiting. "I remember I was being recruited by Ara Parseghian," Zelina recalls. "I was being recruited by every school in the country. I actually said 'No' to Ara in his office. Woody made me feel like he cared about me as a person. He never lied to me and he never promised me anything other than an education and the opportunity to play at one of the best institutions in the country.

"Other coaches were promising me everything from never having to worry about transportation to a new wardrobe. One coach even said he was praying every morning, saying mass, and I know he never saw the inside of a church. But Woody was different. He really cared about the family. He surrounded himself with quality young men. What kind of family a young man was from had a lot of bearing on how hard he went after certain players."

Zelina believes his former coach was a misunderstood man. "Unfortunately, Woody's career ended on a sour note, but I honestly believe that never diminished our respect for the man. I'm sure it affected how the public viewed Woody, but as he would say, 'I don't give a damn what other people think.' The people who knew him, who shared a part of their [lives] with him, love him and respect him. I wish everybody could have had the opportunity to know Woody Hayes . . . to know him as we players knew him. We'd never have to worry about what people think about Woody Hayes. For me, it was a thrill to play for Woody."

*   *   *

The intensity. The drive for perfection. The penchant for preparation. Those were Woody Hayes hallmarks, says Rex Kern, the Buckeyes' quarterback from 1968 to 1970.

"With Woody, the will to win was not as important as the will to prepare to win," he says. "And yes, sometimes he overprepared, usually for Michigan games, to the point of being too fearful."

Regardless, in Kern's eyes Hayes was and remains unsurpassable. "Woody was a great teacher and a great educator," Kern says. "That's the amazing thing . . . what the Old Man could talk about. He was such a well-versed individual, whether it was the arts or literature or politics. Woody was just astounding."

Today, Kern manages his business interests, dividing his time between homes in Columbus and California. He and his wife, Nancy, are the parents of grown sons. To illustrate just how complete the Woody Hayes Experience can be, consider this: Rex and Nancy met in Pasadena, California, where Nancy was a Rose Bowl princess and Rex the self-assured field general who marshaled Ohio State to an undefeated season, the Rose Bowl victory against the University of Southern California, and the national championship in 1968. Magic then, magic now.

In the beginning, one of the most celebrated quarterbacks in OSU history wasn't all that secure about his chances of signing on with the Buckeyes. ". . . Woody didn't recruit me that much," Kern remembers. "He would talk to the principal, my high school football coach. He'd

A familiar sight: quarterback Rex Kern (No. 10) tries to make a point with Woody Hayes as the coach emphasizes his own wishes. Photo courtesy of Ohio State University Sports Information Department.

go to my dad's barbershop and get his hair cut. When he talked to me, it would be about life and the vital importance of getting an education. When I agreed to go to Ohio State . . . my first recollection is of Woody saying, 'Great. I'm excited. Now, here's a list of kids I need you to call and get them to come to The Ohio State University.' He had me on the phone right then and there. I just started calling."

Many credit Hayes with influencing their personal and professional lives. Kern, in a way, does as well, but he says the coach really didn't influence his personal life. "But he built upon the foundation on which my parents raised me. I don't think at age 18 you can reshape one's personality. But he went a long, long way in reinforcing the values that my parents instilled in me."

When it came to football, Kern truly was in his element. Born to lead, he pounced when the opportunity presented itself. "Before my first game my sophomore year, Woody told me I was going to start," Kern says. "Remember, now, I was replacing a two-year letterman, Billy Long. About all Woody told me was, 'You're in charge. . . . Go with your gut.'"

And so Kern did as Hayes instructed. "One game that season, there were about two minutes left in the first half and we had the ball, fourth-and-10. Mike Sensibaugh, a great defensive back who was our punter, came onto the field and I waved him off and called a play," he says.

"Well, the play broke down, but I was able to run for 16, 17 yards and a first down. It's a good thing, too, because if I hadn't made that first down, I might still be running! Actually, I knew what our supporting cast could do; we had a tremendous amount of talent."

Hayes and Kern enjoyed a close relationship on and off the field until the day Hayes died. It was built on trust, honesty, loyalty, integrity, and love.

"I remember the week of the Michigan game, I was pretty tired," Kern remembers. "I walked into the locker room for practice one day and our quarterback coach, George Chaump, says to me, 'Rex, you look pretty tired.' And I said to George, 'Well, I've been in classes from 8:00 until 3:00, I haven't had any lunch. . . . Can you get [me] something?'

"I got dressed [for practice], went out on the field and did calisthenics. [Out of nowhere] a manager comes through the gates holding a McDonald's bag. Lo and behold! Woody grabs me, tells me to go off to the side and eat, then come back in. So I'm sitting there watching and eating, and then I did jump right back in. Woody said to me, 'Rex, if it were anyone else, I'd have 'em eat grass.' And this was during Michigan week!"

Hayes granted Kern considerable freedom, if that's what one would call it, in running the OSU offense for three seasons. "Whether it was an option, sprint-out, dive, draw, pass . . . he gave me greater latitude. That was almost unheard of. I think because of the preparation we did together, it gave me, and the Old Man, the confidence that I could do it," Kern says.

"I guess talent allows you to do a lot of things. You can make mistakes and still look good. We had so many skilled athletes, great leadership, and great talent. Woody used to tell us, 'If you're going to get better, stay focused.' The Old Man worked us to death!"

After Kern's playing days were over, but before he left the university, he worked in the athletic department. Having had Hayes drum into him and every other player on the squad the importance of education, Kern decided to see just how well he and his former lettermen paid attention.

"I did a survey on players who played his first 25 years," Kern remembers. "Eighty-seven point six percent who earned a 'Varsity 0' had graduated. And 37 of those went on to grad school!"

Imagine Kern's glee over the chance to show Hayes the impressive figures. "When I found that out, I thought, 'Man this is really exciting.' I went to Woody and told him. He squinted, pulled on the right side of his glasses and said, 'You're kidding me! I thought it was better than that!' He burst my bubble. And I remember thinking to myself, I pity the brain coach. . . . He's going to be all over him."

Hayes was one of a kind, Kern believes. "He worked harder than anybody. He wouldn't accept less than your best," Kern says. "Fundamentally, Woody was a taskmaster. He'd say, 'Do the small things and the big things, and the games will take care of themselves.' It shouldn't surprise anyone he was so good for so long."

* * *

Woody Hayes did more for Calvin Murray after Hayes' coaching days were over than at anytime during the two seasons Murray, a gifted running back, played under the legendary coach at Ohio State.

Murray, who later played for the Philadelphia Eagles, went to Ohio State from Woodbine, New Jersey, where he was a talented, but underappreciated, multisport star. The football coaching staff at Woodbine, Murray says, didn't do much, if anything, to help him move on to college. As a matter of fact, it was quite the opposite, he says.

"My coaches in high school were prejudiced against all blacks," says Murray. "It seemed they tried to do everything they could to hold me back. When it came time to do the [Scholastic Aptitude Test], the coaches told me not to worry about anything, that it was no big deal because I already had my scholarship [to Ohio State]. So I went in and just started filling in the [test] form. I just made the dots look pretty. I actually believed those guys. The same thing happened to one of my teammates, Bubba Green, who went to North Carolina State and then to the Baltimore Colts.

"Later, when I reported for fall camp at Ohio State, Larry Romanoff, the academic advisor, came over to me and gave me a form to fill out. I did it, and he said, 'Calvin, how did you do that? We thought, you know, because of your test scores. . . .'

"Anyway, during high school the whole time I was on the field I kept thinking to myself I was blessed by God and I'm going to get to where I want to go. One game, I scored six touchdowns in high school."

It must have made quite an impression on the opposing school's coach, because when Hayes' assistant, George Chaump, went to the high school to talk about recruits, the coach ended up telling him about this kid, Calvin Murray, who lit him up six times in one game. The coach showed Chaump film of the game. So Chaump went down to Woodbine, and the rest is Buckeye history.

"In my senior season at Ohio State, and this was two years after Woody had been fired, Woody gave a speech at my high school. The auditorium was packed with kids and parents, and he said to them after this tremendous speech, 'I want you to know this,' and he looks at the high school's coaching staff, 'I'm not here because of you. I'm here because of my boy, to support my son.'"

That's the way Murray remembers Hayes, as a committed, dedicated, family- and education-oriented man who put nothing before his family and team.

With education, Hayes got a jump on all the professors and instructors who were about to take in his freshmen football players.

"There was a class called Word Power, and Woody taught it," Murray remembers. "It was mandatory. Woody taught us English every day at 6:00 [in the morning]. It was a class you didn't miss. Ever. You know what? The lowest grade among the freshmen who were taking English was a 2.7. Who [among coaches] would do this today?"

Murray says Hayes knew many of the professors on campus, and if a player failed to show for a class, Hayes would get a call. Murray says, even though it's typical of a college student to want to blow off class once in a while, it was much, much easier to go to class than deal with the consequences of skipping.

Practices, Murray says, could be grueling. And sometimes the players would be vocal in their complaints. On one occasion, Murray says, Hayes overheard someone complaining about sore legs. "So he decided to call off practice. Just like that. He asked us to go in, shower and dress, then come out and get on the bus. When we did, he had the bus driver take us down to Children's Hospital. Woody made sure we got to see all those poor kids, some of whom would never come out, others with burned limbs or terrible diseases. It made us think twice about never complaining again, and he showed us all we have a lot to be thankful for."

Murray says he recalls his two years playing for Hayes as a sort of military tour of duty. "It seemed as if I was in the armed forces," he says, adding it wasn't all hand-to-hand combat. There was a lot of history mixed in.

"Whenever we would travel to another school for an away game, Woody would take us on a walk through their campus. He'd point out all the historical facts about the school, show us important sites, and then take us into their student union so we could see all the things [posted on bulletin boards] that had been written about us and how they were going to beat us. What a great tactic in motivation!"

There were other times Murray was left scratching his head in puzzlement. "Woody beat himself up many a time, and I never could understand that. He'd go crazy and really smash himself hard. One time I called home and said, 'Dad, come and get me. This man is crazy.' Of course, I stayed. It was a strange way of motivating a team, though."

But the vast majority of the memories are rich for Murray. He recounts how one never knew who would show up at one of the team's practices. "You remember who dotted the *i* in Script Ohio at homecoming in 1978? It was Bob Hope. He used to come to practice. So did former President Nixon and all kinds of generals. Jack Nicklaus would come, too. And Woody would always stop practice and tell us stories about the people who were visiting, and we always liked that because it gave us a break," Murray says with a laugh.

Murray also tells the story of a flight to State College, Pennsylvania, during a snowstorm. The Buckeyes were to play Penn State University the next day. As two propeller-driven planes made their way to the mountaintop landing strip, "Woody had our pilot radio the other pilot, who was flying the plane with the number twos, to tell him to land first. He said, 'If the twos can make it in there, then we'll know it's OK to go in,'" Murray says, again with a chuckle.

Of all the memories—which include touring an aircraft carrier with Hayes in Jacksonville, Florida; how the Old Coach used to sleep at the North Facility, the better to be close to work; how Hayes tried to play every player on the roster during home games; how, when he'd get up at 2:00 in the morning, he'd hear Hayes' projector whirring away in the room next door in the dormitory—one particularly humorous recollection brings forth a belly laugh from Murray.

"Did anyone ever tell you about the showers?" he asks. "Coach Hayes believed he and the coaching staff should shower with the players as a sign of camaraderie. Well, because he couldn't reach his back, someone always had to soap up Woody's back for him. Usually when we saw him coming into the shower, many of us would leave—some still covered with soap—but there'd be some big lineman there rinsing his hair and all of a sudden, there's Woody. And he has to wash his back for him!"

The more serious side of his time with Hayes is what really has made an impact on Murray, though.

"There's not many people who spent as much time with people less fortunate than Woody. Not that I know of, anyway," Murray says. "He did it out of love. He called that 'paying forward.'"

Murray has carried that forward, working in prisons with his Young Men of Destiny organization. He tries to do his part to shape the prisoners so that when they are paroled they'll be better men.

Remembering the last time Murray saw Hayes, he says what struck him most was the coach's powerful and deep memory.

"My dad and I went to his office in the ROTC building one day. Woody's eyesight was failing him," Murray recalls. "But he remembered our voices and he called me by name. Then, and this is what was amazing, he called my dad by his name. It had been a lot of years. It seems he always—and this isn't just me—he always remembered those who were important to him. We were all like family, Woody and Anne and the players.

"I remember seeing Anne at his funeral, and she came up to me and said, 'Hi, Cal. How are you doing?' On the day of her husband's funeral! That's the type of woman she is, and that's why Woody was the type of man he was. She really helped to guide coach Hayes. She was proof that behind every successful man is a good and wonderful woman," says Murray, who, with his wife, Jeri, has six children. "I know that's the case in my life."

Murray says he believes Hayes ultimately should be remembered "as someone who cared about his players and people in general, and that he was not a talker, he was a doer! He showed me the right way to go."

* * *

Frank "Moose" Machinsky is a self-styled hick from the hills. That's how this former All–Big Ten tackle, who played for Woody Hayes from 1953 to 1955, sees himself.

But the reality of the situation is that Machinsky is no more a hick than Dennis Rodman is normal.

It's a long way back to the early fifties, Machinsky will tell you. And he never would have landed where he is today were it not for Hayes "staying on my ass."

When he first arrived at Ohio State, Machinsky was known to enjoy his beer and had an equal appetite for chasing women. As a result, he says, his grades went south. That's all it took. His coach was on him immediately.

"I was living in a fraternity house at the time, and Woody shows up one day and says, 'That's it. Pack your bags. Get your books. You're coming with me.' That's just the way it happened," Machinsky says.

So, doing as he was told, Machinsky gathered his possessions and got into Hayes' car. From the frat house, Hayes drove his player to the coach's home in Upper Arlington. "And he wouldn't let me leave until my grades improved," Machinsky says. "He made me live with him, and he'd come home every night and check my assignments and work. He'd get involved [tutoring] where it was necessary, but more than anything he stayed on me.

"I was always borderline as a student. If it hadn't been for him kicking me in the ass, who knows? No matter the time of night when he got home, he was always going over my work. No doubt about it. If it wasn't for Woody staying after me, I would've flunked out of school. But I got my grades up—I didn't set any records, but I graduated on time."

And that's when Machinsky first learned about the Woody Hayes work ethic. It was widespread, too. For instance, Machinsky remembers when the team would gather for preseason drills. It meant staying in the dorms on the west side of Ohio Stadium.

"I got up one night to take a leak, and as I go down the hall to use the restroom, I passed Woody's room," Machinsky says. "And I could hear that damned projector going at 3:00 in the morning. He was doing film in the middle of the night!"

Preparedness was what Hayes was all about. Not coincidentally, it also is what Machinsky is all about. "When I go into a meeting, goddamn it, I'm ready!" he says, sounding somewhat like his former

Moose Machinsky, who credits Woody Hayes for his work ethic, says had it not been for Hayes, he wouldn't have succeeded in school. Photo courtesy of Ohio State University Sports Information Department.

coach. "Every little detail is taken care of. Just like Woody. It'd drive you nuts, but preparation takes a lot of work. You have to know what you're doing. Woody did, and it rubbed off."

Machinsky forged a tight bond with Hayes and his wife. Anne and Woody used to go to the Machinsky home for Thanksgiving almost every year, Moose says. And he says he's still extremely close to Anne. "I'd do anything for Woody, and I'd do anything for Anne. They were so good to me. If it wasn't for them . . ."

After Hayes died and the home in Upper Arlington became too much for Anne to maintain, she moved to a smaller dwelling. When it came time for the big move, she took what she wanted, "which wasn't much," Machinsky says. "Their son, Steve, took some things. But really, it seemed as if they left everything.

"Being in the garbage business, I helped them throw out what was left. I can't tell you the stuff they threw away! It was unbelievable.

Anne gave me some things, which we auctioned off for charity. But it was load after load after load . . . all of it's gone," he says.

The quintessential Woody story, Machinsky says, centers on a dinner his former players threw for him. The money raised was used to build a cabin for Hayes in the southern Ohio hills.

"We had the dinner at the Sheraton in downtown [Columbus], and they gave me a suite. I was in the beer business at the time, so I went up with case after case of beer and just filled the bathtubs. Anyway, the party got going pretty late and at 3:00 in the morning, Woody takes off. As he's leaving, here come Anne and my wife. They wanted to see all the players, and they ended up staying until 7:00 the next morning."

After the cabin was built, Machinsky and some former players attended to some detail work, including pouring a rock driveway. Hayes asked to pay for the odds and ends the former players were doing. Machinsky would have none of it.

"Actually, we were a little bit short of funds at the time, and Woody found out about it," Machinsky says. "He brought me a check, and I told him, 'Woody, we've got this covered.' And he says, 'Bullshit! I want to pay for it.' And so we went back and forth, and I finally told him how much the guys wanted to do this for him. It didn't matter to him at the time; he wanted to pay. He grabbed me by the shirt and said, 'Goddamn it! Take the check!' And I said, 'Woody, I don't want to fight you.'

"So I ripped up his check right in front of him. But he decided he wanted a picket fence around the cabin. So before he could get it, I called the lumberyard and told the guy to sell him the fence for something like 40 bucks and we'd make up the difference. Woody felt he was paying for something!"

Machinsky and others, in a salute to their late coach's love for education and the military, in the spring of 1997 completed raising money for a $1.25 million chair. It is known as the W. W. Hayes Chair in Strategic Studies. That's known as paying forward, one of Hayes' favorite practices.

Hayes had a knack for understanding the human side of situations, Machinsky says. "Woody caught me with a case of beer after we won the Rose Bowl for the national championship," Machinsky recalls. "It wasn't open, but he wasn't happy, either.

"The next year, Kenny Vargo and I were elected cocaptains of the team and we were having dinner at the Faculty Club with Woody. We talked a little about the season, and then Woody said, 'Kenny, you're excused.' So it's just Woody and me sitting there and he says to me, 'OK, goddamn it, promise me you won't drink any more beer.' And I said, 'I can't.' And he said, 'What?' And I tell him that I've been drinking beer since I was five years old. It was like a ritual with my father. When we had the money, he'd go out for a beer and take me along. I didn't know any other way. I promised Woody I'd still work hard and play hard, but I couldn't make any no-beer promises. So Woody looked at me and finally said, 'OK, goddamn it. But be careful. And don't go . . . where they can see you.'"

Machinsky says Hayes probably was the biggest part of his life for a time, and to this day the coach remains a profound influence on the former player's life. "He was so honorable and honest," Machinsky says. "He was the greatest."

*　*　*

Paul Warfield says Woody Hayes equipped him and his fellow players at Ohio State for success. Not on the football field, but in life.

Warfield, a successful sportswear company executive in south Florida, says Hayes epitomized what *coach* meant. "He saw the mission, yes, to win football games, but more importantly to see that we were educated, that we would be able to compete in the real world and take our places in and make contributions to society," Warfield says. "He wanted to make sure that we would do all we could to make this world a better place in which to live."

Warfield says his coach was not the least bit concerned with developing his players for future roles in the National Football League. He was consumed, Warfield says, by a passion for education.

"Woody Hayes came from a family of educators. His father was a superintendent of schools," the Pro Football Hall of Fame inductee

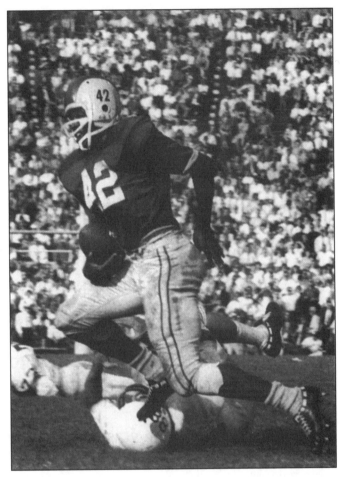

Paul Warfield, who says Woody Hayes "knew everything," eludes the defense for a big gain.
Photo courtesy of Chance Brockway.

recalls. "He had a very keen appreciation of education, and his ultimate concern was that we [players] received our diplomas. Then, it was to win games, the Big Ten championship, and the national championship. And, finally, he instilled in us an overriding sense of loyalty to the state of Ohio."

Among Hayes' other attributes that impressed a young Warfield between 1961 and 1963 was the coach's commitment to work and to those he cared for—and the boundary of that circle was quite wide when one stood at the middle, as Hayes did.

"Woody Hayes was an individual who would not make excuses and who would not let his players make excuses," Warfield says, taking note of Hayes' penchant for hard work and attending to detail.

"He believed if young men put forth the effort and prepared, in most instances they were going to attain success."

Warfield tells the story of a former Buckeye player who went to medical school in the East. The player was having a rough go of it in school and was having second thoughts. He had arrived at the decision to abandon his quest to become a doctor. But before he gave up, he called Hayes. "As the story goes, he wanted coach Hayes to hear it straight from him, not from another source," Warfield says. "And Woody told the young man, 'I don't want you to do that. . . . I don't want you to do anything for the next three hours.'

"And with that, Woody Hayes left the staff meeting he was in, went to Port Columbus, got on an airplane, and flew out there. He convinced the young man to stay, and the young man went on to become a doctor and still may be having a stellar medical career. Woody Hayes was always willing to extend a helping hand."

Warfield also remembers how his coach helped an inner calm to prevail in the wake of "that ill-fated Friday in November 1963" when President John F. Kennedy was fatally wounded by gunfire as his motorcade made its way through Dallas.

The Ohio State football team was in Ann Arbor, Michigan, to play the Wolverines in the season finale. Warfield recounts the chain of events. "We were in our hotel, and I was relaxing in my room with my roommate, Matt Snell," Warfield says. "We had the TV on, and the report from Dallas comes on about President Kennedy. The story became more dreadful as time went on, and then Walter Cronkite announced the president was dead. For me, the memory is of a football team, and an entire nation, that was just stunned.

"Woody Hayes announced that the game the next afternoon was canceled and that we'd play it the following weekend. There was a great sense of wonderment in the room. But Woody Hayes had the capacity and ability to put everything into perspective."

Warfield says Hayes "knew everything." He remembers the coach holding an hour-long team meeting, during which he extolled the virtues of the U.S. government and the nation itself. He reassured his players that there was nothing to be alarmed about, that theirs was a great nation and life, somehow, would go on.

Hayes, whom Warfield characterizes as possibly the lowest-paid and most successful coach of his era, was a man "who loved doing his job, who loved The Ohio State University, and who loved working with young people."

Warfield remembers his coach "as a giant, a man who was committed to young men who could make a better society." He remembers Hayes as the coach who concerned himself "with the development of his young men, who would make the state of Ohio the best state and the United States the best nation."

And from Woody Hayes, Paul Warfield learned, and to this day employs, "hard work, sacrifice, and dedication."

* * *

Late in the spring of 1984, the Oakland Invaders of the old United States Football League were practicing for an upcoming game. The practice happened to coincide with a visit to the San Francisco Bay area by Woody Hayes.

The Oakland coach at the time was Chuck Hutchison, a former offensive lineman for Ohio State from 1967 to 1969. He was Hayes' host for the engagement, and unbeknownst to the former player, the Old Coach had shown up at practice.

"I didn't know he was coming," Hutchison remembers. "We were in the middle of a seven-on-seven passing drill and had been going at it for 20 minutes when Woody walks out onto the field. I didn't see him, but I could sense that something was brewing. The players were acting a little strange, with weird looks on their faces.

"Then all of a sudden, it's 'Oh, shit! What am I doing wrong?' Everything he used to hate about coaches I didn't want to violate. Did I have my hands in my pockets? Was there anything else?

"He walks over and talks to the team about the things they needed to do. And then he turns to me and says, 'Goddamn it! If you're going to win, you're going to have to run the ball!'"

Hutchison, as politely as he could and with no small amount of edginess, explained to his coach that it was just a passing drill. As all this was going on, Hutchison says, "you could've heard a pin drop. [The players] were in awe, and maybe a little afraid. They had heard of the legend of Woody Hayes. Their reaction was truly remarkable."

Later that night, at the banquet where Hayes was the featured speaker, Hayes made his way to the lectern.

"Well, Chuck, I don't know why you're here. You're not going to win any games listening to me. As a matter of fact, I can't believe you won any games," Hayes said, bringing down the house.

Hutchison had taken over an Oakland team that had opened the season 0–3, then promptly lost the next five games for the new coach before reeling off seven consecutive victories (for *another* new coach) to end the season. Maybe it was Hayes' presence at the practice. Nobody knows. What Hutchison knows, though, is that Woody Hayes had a profound influence on his personal and professional lives.

"He had the ability to stay with things until he achieved his goal, and that's admirable," Hutchison remembers. "And he learned something from almost everybody he came in contact with. He'd just continue to ask a person a series of questions, probably until he felt he had learned something. And he *always* remembered."

Hutchison says he believes Hayes probably found himself to be boring. "I don't think he ever could understand what all the fuss was about. I think he held himself in high esteem, but it wasn't anything he wanted to spend any time talking about. He could captivate an audience. Let me tell you, that night when Woody was the main speaker at the banquet in San Francisco, nobody—I mean nobody—expected him to be like that."

And that is another facet of the coach that Hutchison found intriguing. "He was not a predictable man except in one way," the former National Football League veteran recalls. "If Woody Hayes put his mind to it, there wasn't much he couldn't accomplish. And putting your mind to it, in his eyes, was more important than the accomplishment."

Hutchison says Hayes taught him how to earn his stripes. He learned humility, about getting one's butt kicked and being able to keep everything in perspective.

"It was that way with education," Hutchison says. "My freshman year, I had a horrible first quarter with my grades. Woody came up to me and said, 'Son, have another quarter like that and you won't be with us. Do you understand?' Well, it was the first time I had ever been under that kind of microscope.

"We had a $5 bet that I'd get a 3.0 [grade average] or better. And every 10 days to two weeks he'd call me or come up to me and ask me how I was doing. Of course, you know, he knew how everything was going at the time. Well, I ended up with a 3.1 and won the $5.

"See, he truly cared about every player. Later, when my sister was at Ohio State, he used to call her just to see how she was doing. The man was incredible."

Hutchison says Hayes' recollection of people was legendary. "He would speak to every [player's] family, and he could remember them on a first-name basis," Hutchison says. "Something like that doesn't register at the time, and you don't appreciate it right away, but you were in his thoughts day to day. For Woody, things intuitively or instinctively came to mind."

What Hutchison believes made Hayes a successful coach is that he never minimized anything. If you listened, if you believed, there would be validation somewhere along the line.

"My senior year we went to an audible system," Hutchison recalls. "We could call plays at the line. He figured if we could run 75 plays in 10 to 15 seconds each, we'd score more and win. He was right. We used that my whole senior year. We ran formations with motion and with color codes. And we changed the color codes every week. There's no way any team could scout us."

Hutchison says there were times he'd just as soon forget, including the appearance by the Big Ten Skywriters at a preseason practice before his senior season. The Skywriters were an assemblage of media that flew from campus to campus in the Big Ten, compiling preseason stories on each team.

"When the Skywriters were there, I jumped offside on one play," Hutchison says. "[Woody] stops practice and comes over to me, with all the media there, and says, 'Son, you're the dumbest son of a bitch in the Big Ten. You're the dumbest player I've ever coached.' I was an All–Big Ten candidate at the time, and he singles me out, telling me I don't deserve an Ohio State University jersey.

"It was 250 yards from the practice field back to the training facility, and he made me walk in full view of everybody, not run, all the way back. I was hot. I mean, really mad. Later, Woody comes up to me and says, 'You know why I did that? Because you play better when you're mad. And now you'll have a goddamn great year!'" Hutchison credits his coach with the ability to be ultimately prepared and to maximize the abilities of his players.

"And his values were impeccable. He never compromised," Hutchison says. "He used his values to make the good great, and the great nearly immortal. With Woody, it wasn't just lip service."

And so it goes, Hutchison says, for himself and many of his former teammates. "Even now, he's as big as life," he says. "He lives in every one of us. From Woody Hayes, all of us learned something that made a difference in our lives."

* * *

Steve Luke, the former "200 pounds, soaking wet" center turned defensive back, says Woody Hayes had a major effect on his life.

"The thing that is truly remarkable is that I've never met anybody that's had a more positive influence . . . in a special way, outside of Jesus Christ, than Woody Hayes. I had my father, but my father died when I was growing up. Woody was almost like a second father to me," says Luke, who played at OSU from 1972 through 1974.

"I met Woody when I was 17. I always felt that we had a special relationship. Woody and I spent some good, quality time together. He was always there with an ear, and he always gave good advice. Woody Hayes was the most honest person I've met. You always knew where you stood with Woody."

Luke says the one thing he appreciates to this day about Hayes "was that he gave me an opportunity, which is what he promised me when he recruited me. He asked me to play center, and you've got to remember that Woody liked small centers; they were quick and could get to the linebackers. I was 200 pounds, soaking wet. He decided they'd utilize my quickness."

At that time, he was competing with Steve Myers, who went on to become a decorated center for the Buckeyes. "Steve Myers and I are great

Former OSU standout defensive back Steve Luke credits Woody Hayes with never being outworked. Here, the legendary coach busies himself with a page from a game plan. Photo courtesy of Ohio State Sports Information Department.

friends. We came in [to Ohio State] together, and we competed against each other. We all want to start, and I ended up starting my sophomore year, because Steve got mononucleosis, and I ended up starting the Rose Bowl. The spring going into my junior year, Woody asked me to switch to defensive back after one practice. I was upset because I thought, in my mind, that I had given Steve Myers a run for his money. . . . I was a little bent out of shape.

"I called my mom, and she reminded me that I was there for one thing, and that was to get an education. And she issued a challenge to me: 'It's not always gonna be easy, and just because it's difficult doesn't mean you can't lick it.'"

It helped to bring some perspective to his situation. But Luke says the Old Coach also played a major role.

"Woody was instrumental in me graduating on schedule. My last quarter, I had to take 24 hours to graduate on schedule. I wasn't sure I wanted to do that," Luke says. "But Archie [Griffin, Luke's roommate] told me his brother did it. I still was debating, and I ran into Woody. He asked what I was going to do and I said I was still debating. And he said, 'Remember that promise we made your mom!' The thing that scared me was he actually remembered the conversation in the living room of our apartment. He even remembered the boxes in the living room, because we had just bought some furniture. This was four years later! Do you know how many people he saw between the time it happened and [that day]? I went back and I told Archie, 'You're right. I'm going to do it.'"

The one-time roommates later were best men at each other's weddings. Hayes fostered that, the reliance on good people. And good people were the ones who would work "their fannies" off, leaving nothing to chance.

"Woody used to say that he may not be the smartest, that there may be people luckier than him, but no one's ever gonna outwork him," Luke says. "I took that philosophy and incorporated that in my life.

"Woody also used to say things like, 'You can't start reading the papers.' And, 'If anyone pats you on the back, be careful because you'll get a knife in it.' I use that philosophy in business. I always feel that I have to turn it up and work harder."

Luke, the former All–Big Ten defensive back, says he employs another Hayes axiom: "I have the understanding that you have to practice what you preach. Just like Woody did.

"For years his staff was the lowest paid. Why? Because he refused to take a pay raise. It was his way of fighting inflation. When I first went to Woody's house, I recognized that it was a nice house, but he could've had something bigger or better. There's a world of difference between the house Woody Hayes lived in and the one [former OSU coach] John Cooper has. Material things were not important to

Woody. He'd tell us that you don't judge a person by what he has, but by what he is."

Pressed for a favorite anecdote from his years as a Buckeye, Luke laughs heartily as he launches, seemingly breathlessly, into this: "Archie and I were roommates. When they moved me to defensive back, it was his freshman year and he had established himself. So I'm a defensive back and they give him the ball on a pitch during practice one day, and here's my shot. It was during the spring, and I figured that if I could get in one good shot on Archie, that'll catch Woody's eye and it'll enhance my chances. So here comes Archie and I'm barreling toward him, just ready to get in a good lick and he steps out [of bounds]. I still gave him a good lick, and all I hear is, 'You idiot! You idiot! You idiot! You're trying to kill our best back!'

"He sent me off the field; it was incredibly embarrassing, but I learned a valuable lesson. Archie didn't talk to me for two months. He was mad, Woody was mad, and here I am thinking, I just blew everything up in one shot."

Luke didn't get mad, though. He prefers to remember it as getting even—as much as you can get even with your good buddy.

"In Archie's first year at Cincinnati, his first game of the exhibition season was against Green Bay [for which Luke played for six seasons]. They ran him on the same play as that day in [spring] practice. I ran up to him and tried to deck him. I stood over him and said, 'Welcome to the NFL, you rookie.' He ended up scoring two touchdowns that game, but they weren't over me.

"See, the one thing Woody would always respect was hard work. So I came right back. I came out and kept my nose to the grind, and in all the years I played football I never, ever missed a practice.

"Anyway, Archie said, 'Luke I don't know why Woody loves you.' As I said, it was a very special relationship."

Luke says Woody knew how to win with people. "He knew he was a master at knowing people and knowing what hot buttons to hit and how to get inside your head. No one wanted to be an AYO [All You Others], but Woody always respected their role with the team.

"Woody Hayes recognized quality. You knew you were going to be challenged. Those kinds of challenges build character. And Woody's going to play the best person. He may not be the best athlete, but he'll be the best person. All he wanted was for you to give your best . . . not more than he was giving."

Luke recalls having just beaten the University of Michigan in 1974. The Buckeyes were in the locker room, and Hayes was at his postgame best. Someone in the room announced to the coach that the president was on the phone. "They'll have to wait. I'm talking to my men." Woody kept President Gerald Ford at bay (maybe because he was a Michigan alum?), and, as Luke remembers it, "A couple of minutes later when he was done talking to us, he said, 'I'll take that call.'"

Hayes' acts of kindness are embedded in Luke's memory, too.

"There was another player, an AYO player, that had hurt his knee two days before the Michigan game in 1974. He was in the hospital and Woody went by to see the kid either Thursday or Friday evening before the game. This kid was an AYO, I don't remember who, but he was a hard-working kid. You got Michigan coming in a few hours, this kid isn't a factor at all in the game plan, and Woody's visiting the kid in the hospital!"

Luke, who operates an athlete representation company in Columbus, prefers to remember Woody Hayes as "a fighter for the right things. He was adamant about always doing the right thing. And when he gave speeches, they'd pay him and he'd give the money to charity. He preached about paying forward. That allowed me to grow in so many ways. I still make mistakes, but I do know that there's a difference between right and wrong, and as long as I continue to do the right thing everything works out."

* * *

Steve Myers says the Woody Hayes he remembers was the man who never stopped short of sticking up for his players as individuals and as a team.

What crystallized that feeling for Myers, an All-America center for the Buckeyes in 1974, was a postgame incident at East Lansing, Michigan, during the 1974 season.

"Here we are, the number one team in the country, playing at Michigan State and Levi Jackson rips off an 88-yard touchdown run," Myers recalls. "We're down [16–13], but we get the ball back and drive all the way down the field, and we're confident. We were ready for that situation. Every Thursday, we'd practice our goal-line offense for 20 minutes. We had referees there, too. Hell, we could run five plays in 30 seconds with no timeouts, and we could score every time.

"So [at MSU], Champ Henson gets the ball on the goal line and we think he scores to give us the win. It sounded like [the public-address announcer] said we won, and there was so much noise. Then we thought we heard him say we lost. All I know is that one official signaled touchdown. And he was the only one left on the field [after time ran out]; the others took off, and I don't blame them. It wasn't until we got into the locker room there that we found out we had definitely lost."

And that was the start of something really big for Myers and his teammates. "When Woody got confirmation that we had, indeed, lost, that was it. He picked up a chair and shattered it into about 60 pieces. He was ranting and raving, and the doctors kept telling him to calm down, because he'd had that heart attack the year before. And he yells at them, 'F*** my heart!' And then he throws his heart pills on the floor and starts stomping on them."

After a moment, Hayes apparently had regained his composure. He turned to his stunned players, his ire raising faster than desert sand in a windstorm, and announced: "You motherf***ers like to fight, don't you? Let's go kick their asses!"

Myers said the players snapped to attention and lined up behind Hayes. "So we're there, about 60 of us versus their, what, 120?" Myers says. "And we start walking across the hall to their locker room. And in the hallway is [then–Big Ten commissioner] Wayne Duke.

"Well, Woody just throws Wayne Duke up against the wall. I mean he throws him. And he says to Duke, 'Tell my team they got f***ed.'

And Wayne Duke says, 'Woody, they got f***ed.' And Woody says, 'All right fellas, let's get on the bus.'

"So we get out to the buses, and there was a huge crowd there, probably most of [Michigan State's] fans. And they start rocking the bus I'm on. Next thing you know, Woody's telling the bus driver, 'F*** 'em. Run 'em over.'"

Well, it never came to pass that Spartans fans were run over by Woody's bus, but Myers says the coach would do anything to help or stand behind his players, seemingly anywhere, anytime. "I know that he found out that a former player's wife was suffering from brain cancer and the medical insurance had just about run out," Myers says. "So, Woody agreed to be roasted, with all the money going to help pay the leftover medical bills for this woman.

"And another time I was back in Columbus and I went up to his office to visit him. We talked a little, and then his secretary says she has a call for him from a woman whom he does not know, but whose daughter was hospitalized with cancer."

Hayes quickly took the call, Myers says, and the next thing anyone knows, the two are strolling out of his office, with Hayes telling his secretary he was leaving and wouldn't be back that day. "So we got in my car and I drove him over to the practice facility. He had [equipment manager] John Bozick give him six or seven footballs and all kinds of OSU football stuff," Myers says. "And then we're off to Children's Hospital to visit the girl.

"Well, when we got there, you could tell it meant everything to the girl, and all the kids there just went berserk. We stayed there for three or four hours. And Woody was just great to those kids. He did that stuff all the time, and it was always [Hayes saying], 'I don't want to read about this in the paper, do you understand?' He was that private about the things he did for people."

But Myers wants to be public about his appreciation for the things Woody Hayes did for him, chief among them "staying on my butt" about graduating from Ohio State. When he was finished with pro football, Myers was making a living selling rustproofing systems to automobile dealerships in Illinois.

"And every six weeks, like clockwork, he'd call me up and get on me about not having graduated," Myers says. "I mean, here I am, selling rustproofing. My eligibility's used up. I can do absolutely nothing for this man."

Except graduate. "Get your ass back in school," Hayes told Myers.

He did, with a lot of assistance from Hayes, who helped to arrange a job for Myers so he could pay for the classes he needed to graduate.

"He always told me, 'You owe it to yourself.' And so I finally succumbed to his pressure. I owe him a lot from that standpoint."

Today, Myers is a sales manager for a Chicago-area steel company. A resident of Crown Point, Indiana, he is married and is the father of four children. In his job and in his life, Myers practices what Hayes long ago preached about taking care of your own, being honest, and understanding the real value in and of education.

"You know, it really doesn't sink in until you're gone from there for a while," Myers says. "But Woody had tremendous motivation and he was tremendous at motivating. I owe a lot to him."

* * *

Neal Colzie had just entered another world when he arrived in Columbus from Coral Gables, Florida. He had been the best of the best at Coral Gables High School, an all-state selection in football, basketball, and baseball. But once he landed at Ohio State as yet another prized recruit of Woody Hayes, he was just another player, another number.

He quickly learned that there were others like him, that he was just one of many, and Hayes wouldn't let him think otherwise.

"Woody the coach was a lot like Woody the person," said Colzie, the 1974 All-America defensive back and former standout with the Oakland Raiders, Miami Dolphins, and Tampa Bay Buccaneers, before hid death in 2001. "Some people try to BS you, but not Woody. He let you know exactly where he stood . . . and exactly where you stand."

But those early days of Colzie's time at Ohio State were trying. There he was—it might as well have been a million miles from home—

in a climate vastly different, culturally and otherwise, and fending for himself for the first time in his young life. To his dying day, he adamantly refused to second-guess his decision to attend OSU. He assessed his time there as well spent, but it didn't start out that way, especially his relationship with Hayes.

"Quite naturally, the beginning was tough. First, there was the age difference," Colzie remembered. "Then, there were those of us who'd think, he doesn't know what it's like or what it's about. Hell, you were King Shit at that point in your life. But I thank God to this day that I didn't carry myself that way. Coach Hayes wouldn't let me or any of us."

Colzie toiled under Hayes' watch from 1972 to 1974, earning All-America honors and being named a team captain as a senior. Three consecutive trips to the Rose Bowl for games against the University of Southern California were icing on a 29-4-1 run to which he contributed mightily.

But Colzie carried with him memories vastly different from final scores and individual honors. He said he had been to one football game since 1985, when he retired from the pro game. When he thought back to his days with Hayes, he instantly offered this assessment: "He was the best guy to enter my life, outside of my dad. At 18, without Woody Hayes entering my life, I never would have made it to the next level. You learned so much from coach Hayes, the important things that don't matter in football. He prepared us for life. That's real."

But the football lessons made an impact, too, Colzie said. "After I left coach Hayes, I went on to play for John Madden, Don Shula, and John McKay. They were all bona fide coaches. But what set coach Hayes apart from them and everyone else is this: all coaches talk about getting 110 percent out of their players. The difference? *He* got it."

The grueling practices, the demanding standards, and the no-nonsense approach to football could leave a player to sometimes wonder. Colzie said practices could be unbearable, especially in the late autumn chill—and especially for a kid from a Miami suburb. The whistles, the fits, the swearing.

Woody Hayes remains glued to the action as a TV cameraman moves in for a closer shot during a victory at Michigan. Photo courtesy of Chance Brockway.

"Sure, you'd curse him under your breath. . . . He couldn't tolerate mistakes or breakdowns," Colzie said. "And we as players couldn't always understand how someone could be so wrapped up in it. But none of us disliked coach Hayes, because underneath it all he had no ego and he was a very normal man. He just didn't care what people thought about him.

"He believed, he taught, and he preached. People didn't understand how hard he prepared to win. And if we lost, he'd tell everyone it was *his* fault, not the players'. He put his life on the line every time, and that's what really set him apart."

Colzie remembered being summoned to Hayes' office, "and I get to the office wondering what was waiting. He'd just called me in, and he was watching films. But we never talked about football; it was always about life."

And it was about will, Colzie believed: the will to prepare, the will to succeed, the will to win. Not for or in football, but in life. And when Colzie used to volunteer his time to speak to youth at Miami-area centers, he found himself sounding a lot like the man he once couldn't understand.

"Yes, a lot of the things I do and say reflect coach Hayes. At least I hope so," Colzie said, before a heart attack claimed his life. "To this day, I have the utmost respect for him."

The last time Colzie and Hayes saw each other was in 1985 during the weekend of the season-ending Michigan game in Columbus. "I had come in for the game and I saw coach Hayes," Colzie said. "There was going to be a parade the next day, on Sunday, and he asked me to stay over. So I did, and that was the last time I saw him. And the best part is, the last time I saw him he was smiling."

* * *

Woody Hayes had so much going for him, former player Ted Provost says. "Basically it was respect. I don't know anybody who didn't respect coach Hayes."

Provost, who played defensive back for the Buckeyes from 1967 to 1969, says Hayes was a compassionate man, "always asking how you were doing."

And the former standout defender, who played for a time in the Canadian Football League, also saw the intense side of Hayes. "When I was a freshman in the fall of 1966, I remember him showing up to practice with two black eyes. We all wondered what happened. Well, obviously, he got mad."

Hayes didn't just take out his frustrations on himself. The players were targets, too, Provost says. "I remember I lined up wrong one time during practice, and he slugged me across the side of the head. He was so intense in getting his point across, but it was nothing malicious."

Provost looks back at his days at Ohio State with a sense of accomplishment, and he credits Hayes for that. "When I got there, we went through a building process. My sophomore year, we had three losses, but he slowly built the team into one of the greatest," Provost says. "One year, there were 'Good-bye, Woody' signs, and the next he was the top dog in the world."

What now impresses Provost about his old coach is the way Hayes used to conduct team matters. "For him, it was his way as the only way, and that's how he did things," Provost recalls. "I mean, he never let his players be interviewed unless he was there. If you wrote anything negative about him or his teams you weren't allowed into practice. Paul Hornung [the late sports editor of *The Columbus Dispatch*] was the only one, really, who was allowed into our practices back then."

Provost says he believes Hayes attained such a high level of success for the simple reason that "he was so demanding. He was demanding of his players [and] assistant coaches. There was no slacking off. And, he was a good recruiter, probably the best at getting talent in the state."

The last time coach and player saw each other was at a downtown Columbus parade in Hayes' later years. "He was in a wheelchair then," Provost remembers. "But still, he remembered you. He always knew who you were. He was that way with all the players."

Provost, married and the father of three children, says Hayes should be remembered for his work ethic above all else. The Columbus resident and building contractor says an outgrowth of his relationship with Hayes is something he carries with him daily.

Says Provost, paraphrasing Hayes: "When you encounter tough times, stick to it. And if you do, it'll always work out for the best."

* * *

Ron Ayers knows intensity. As a member of the Ohio State offensive line—as a guard, center, and tight end from 1974 to 1976—he experienced it firsthand. Often.

"I remember Woody Hayes as a very intense coach," Ayers says. "He had a sense of humor, yes, but not about much. He was a perfectionist, mainly."

Ayers says Hayes wanted his players to be the best they could be—regardless of whether it was when they were playing for Ohio State or years later. As so many other players do, Ayers remembers how Hayes talked often not about paying back but about paying forward instead.

"I like to think I pay forward to my community now, whether it's coaching sports or just being involved in other aspects," he says.

Ayers also says some things he learned from Hayes are the very things he tries to pass along to his children. "I try to stress to my kids that nothing in life comes easy," Ayers says. "Anything you get out of life that's any good you have to work hard for."

Ayers says he believes that Hayes was a successful coach because he surrounded himself with top-drawer talent—not only on the roster, but on his coaching staff. "You win with people. That was the title of his book," says Ayers, chuckling. "But it's true. He surrounded himself with great coaches and great players. And great players make great coaches."

Still, there was that quality Hayes always was demanding. "He was a perfectionist. He demanded perfection from you when you came to Ohio State," Ayers remembers. "You expected to win. I ended up in three Rose Bowls and an Orange Bowl. It doesn't get a lot better than that."

Through all the success and good times, there were incidents that made Ayers cringe. "Publicly, he was much different than he was behind the scenes," Ayers recalls. "On the field and in the locker room, he kept things well hidden. The Clemson incident [in the 1978 Gator Bowl] . . . that was no big deal. I saw it every day in practice. He took swings at me, too. It was part of his motivation. He couldn't hurt anyone. But the message was, 'Don't make that mistake again.'"

Was Hayes a fair coach? Ayers says people's answers are diverse.

"When I was there, I don't think he was always fair. Some people who should've played didn't, probably because of the way they dressed or acted," Ayers says. "Do you remember Nick Buonamici? Well, if Nick hadn't taken his earring out, he wouldn't have played. Woody had his favorites . . . just like any[one]."

Ayers, however, to this day has a lot of respect for Hayes. He also has mixed emotions about the way he was used during his days with the Buckeyes. "My whole junior year, I started," Ayers remembers. "As a senior, I was the second-team center. They had moved a kid to center who previously was playing [middle guard] behind Aaron Brown. At the same time, they were recruiting this kid's friend from his old high school in Cincinnati. It was like, 'Hey, your buddy's starting; you can, too, here.' He ended up going to Notre Dame.

"It was kind of a sore spot with me. But they kept telling me that if I kept working hard I would play, and I did."

The Woody Hayes that Ayers remembers also was a stubborn man. Witness the Rose Bowl of 1976. "We were playing UCLA, and we had beaten them [41–20] earlier in the season," he says. "The coaches would tell him we had to change up the game plan. And Woody believed that since we beat them once doing it his way, we could beat them again.

"Dick Vermeil outcoached him that day [in a 23–10 loss]. UCLA knew everything about us. They knew our formations, our tendencies, where the ball was going on any play. We should have won that game."

Still and all, Ayers says, playing for Hayes was a big plus, adding: "It was an experience I wouldn't want to trade."

* * *

In late November 1970, the Buckeyes were girding for their annual season-ending showdown with the University of Michigan. Only 12 months earlier the "team from up north" had ruined a perfect season by upsetting Ohio State.

The Thursday before the 1970 game, Woody Hayes had his troops assemble for practice. They wore sweatpants. It was to be a walk-through for the revenge game.

"I thought we were having a darned good practice," former center Tom DeLeone recalls. "The offense was in a huddle, when all of a sudden

Looking a lot like the man to whom he often is compared—Vince Lombardi—Woody Hayes lets it fly during a home game in the seventies. Photo courtesy of Chance Brockway.

here comes Woody. He pulls off his hat, rips the bill off of it, throws it on the ground, and stomps on it.

"Then, you're not going to believe this, he gets down on all fours. I mean, right in the middle of the huddle! And he starts feeling everyone's feet with his hands. He kept saying, 'I can feel it; you're not ready to win . . . I can feel it; you're not ready to win.' Well, none of us dared look each other in the eye, because we *all* would've cracked."

That's the way it so often went with Hayes, DeLeone says. The man was so totally committed to the game and his team that everything mental and physical was poured into preparation.

"Rex [Kern, the quarterback] was in the huddle with us at the time. Nobody said a word, but his backup, Ron Maciejowski, was about 80 yards down the field rolling around on the ground and laughing like mad. After a few minutes, Woody got up and said, 'Get to work.'"

And that was, by all means, that. End of episode.

DeLeone, a criminal investigator for the U.S. Customs Service and a resident of Park City, Utah, says it was fairly typical. "Discipline was the biggest factor. He demanded it of the players and his assistants. Man, 'Be on time' meant we had to get there 10 minutes early, because the door would be shut 5 minutes early."

The Cleveland Browns veteran says Hayes was always teaching his players, and not always about football.

It started for DeLeone in the family apartment in Kent, Ohio. Hayes had come on a recruiting visit, and DeLeone, the former standout for Kent Roosevelt High School, was all set to talk football.

"He didn't talk about football, not at all," DeLeone says. "It was all about education. That's what he told my mom. He said, 'We'd like to see your son come to Ohio State, and I promise you that if he does he will graduate from Ohio State.'"

And that was only the start of it.

"We were at Illinois, and at the team dinner there was a big portrait of Abraham Lincoln," DeLeone remembers. "As soon as dinner was over, Woody tapped his water glass with a spoon. The room got real quiet. Then for the next hour and a half, he told us all about Abe Lincoln. It was my first time; a lot of the guys had heard it before."

When the Old Coach's mind was on Ohio State football, nothing could cloud it. He wouldn't allow it. Nor would he allow his players any distractions. Says DeLeone: "I remember him calling me in after I'd been elected team captain. He sat me down and said, 'I don't want you thinking about pro football.' Just like that. Out of the blue. And then he said, 'You're going to be a pro football player and you'll be a darned good one. Now, get it out of your mind.' With Woody, you never knew."

DeLeone says the sophomores were afraid of Hayes, the juniors respected him, and the seniors, well, "they just thought he was nuts." The way DeLeone figures it, "you either loved him or you hated him. I loved him."

* * *

Ask Doug Plank about his recollections of Woody Hayes, and he enthusiastically breaks into a litany of stories. At the end of the conversation, you're convinced the longtime Chicago Bears defensive back, for whom Buddy Ryan's 46 defense was named, is ready to strap on the pads and get after it. He, perhaps as much as any of Hayes' former charges, symbolizes what the coach stood for. Foremost in Plank's mind was Woody's unbridled enthusiasm for preparation. Plank says Hayes was fond of saying, "They may outsmart me, but they're never gonna outwork me."

And so it went for the former western Pennsylvania standout running back, who, when he got to Ohio State, was "nothing more than your average white running back. I knew it, they knew it," says Plank, who owns Burger King franchises in the Phoenix area, where he lives with his wife and two children, and in Kansas City.

Still, Hayes and his assistant coaches never gave up on Plank, although they did switch him to defense and promptly placed him on the depth chart . . . as the sixth-team safety.

He never would have made it *that* far, Plank says, had it not been for a knee injury he suffered after enrolling at OSU.

"The injury was a blessing, although at first, when my cartilage started to lock up on me when I was on the scout team, everyone thought I was a hypochondriac. I was always down every three weeks.

"But then it locked up for good, and the doctors said I needed surgery. Let me tell you, it was the best thing that ever happened to me, because it was like someone was saying, 'Doug, you're way underdeveloped in comparison to these guys.' So I really got into lifting weights, and gradually I began to build myself up. I really, I mean really, got into it. I told myself, 'I never want to go back there again.' And I didn't."

Plank says Hayes didn't take to Plank's admitted overly aggressive style of playing defense, but the coach nonetheless elevated his sophomore to second-string safety in 1972.

"Basically, I just played on special teams," Plank recalls. "But I learned the art of tackling and head-butting and spearing. Besides, we were so good that we were always kicking off, so I had a chance to prove myself. And I funneled a whole week's preparation into just four or five plays a game.

"Woody was a rough-and-tumble sort of coach, but he didn't really like my style and he didn't always appreciate it. For instance, we were way ahead of some team, I forget which, and Woody called for the Victory Punt. That's where you're so far ahead that you just punt the ball and do very little else. Normally, my job was to block the contain man. Well, the kid was looking up and here I come. I laid him out right in front of the OSU bench. The whole sideline erupted, but Woody went crazy on me.

"He just embarrassed the heck out of me in front of my teammates. He slapped me in the face a couple of times. It was such humiliation to have that happen in front of the team, and I was only doing what I thought was my job. That's the way I always played."

After three seasons of being a member of the AYOs, or All You Others, Plank was making a serious run at being a starter. There truly was a caste system at Ohio State, Plank says. "There was Red One, the offense. There was The Bucks, the defense. And, of course, there was the AYOs."

So heading into the fall of 1974, Plank was pushing Tim Fox for a starting berth. "If I hiccuped, I was done for," Plank says.

"During one play in practice before the season, I dive to catch a guy and miss him, and the next thing I know I'm out on my feet. It was a concussion. So I ask myself, 'Do I come out? Do I gut it out? Do I not let that kid behind me [on the depth chart] into the huddle?' I decided to stay in, not really knowing where I was. The whole time, I can hear Woody screaming like crazy. He was going insane!

"Well, the next play was the same option play from the 1973 Michigan game. I was half-dazed, failed to rotate [into proper coverage], and there was a deep pass. The guy caught it, and Woody went berserk. He tore up his hat and stomped on it, and his glasses, too. He absolutely unraveled me. He threw me on the ground. He was punching me in the stomach, yelling at me, 'Get the heck out of here.'"

Plank says Dick Walker, Hayes' defensive backfield coach at the time and obviously a master of understatement, wandered over to his player, the one with the stars whirring around his head and chimes going off inside, and said, "You know, you cannot make the same mistake twice."

Says the player, "Here I was going into my senior year with a chance to start, and now I was an AYO again. It was back to special teams for me. The team didn't need Doug Plank to be in there. But then Rich Parsons, one of our safeties, broke his arm and they started me. And let me tell you, they were pained. They put me in at strong safety, and I fit in pretty well.

"Well, it ended up coming down to the Michigan game as it always did, and that's the year we had that great goal-line stand [in a 14–11 OSU victory]. I remember on one of the four plays, it was just me and [Michigan's running back] Chuck Heater, face mask to face mask, and I just flattened him."

Plank and the Buckeyes wended their way westward for the matchup against vaunted tailback Anthony Davis and the University of Southern California. The bottom fell out, again, for Plank during the first Rose Bowl practice on the West Coast. As he was stretching before drills, Hayes and Walker approached him, congratulated him for helping the team get to Pasadena, and told him he was being moved to the kickoff team.

"Let me tell you, it was like a dagger in my chest," Plank says. "I was done. How could this happen? I was determined to go out in a blaze of glory. On one of the kickoffs, I busted the wedge and hit my man so bad that I flattened my face mask. They didn't have another, so they had to tape it together through the ear hole of my helmet.

"Here I was, a senior, in the Rose Bowl and the only senior of the AYOs. Who was gonna want me?"

Months later, he found out. Sitting in his room one day during the National Football League draft, the phone rang. His roommate, tight end Mike Bartozek, answered it. The call was from the Chicago Bears. And the rest was academic. His first season in Chicago, Plank led the Bears in tackles.

"I applied the work habits and work ethic that Woody taught us all. I really credit Woody Hayes. His system was bigger than any one player."

The truth is, Plank never intended to attend Ohio State. He very badly wanted to go to Penn State University, like most of the kids from his area. He said Joe Paterno talked with him after Plank finished playing a high school basketball game, and the coach, "as delicately and eloquently as he could, told me it'd be best if I went to a junior college, built myself up a little, and then reapplied [to Penn State]."

Shortly thereafter, he was in class and heard over the loudspeaker, "Doug Plank, please report to the office."

So he got up and headed for the principal's office, not knowing what to expect and . . . "There was Earle Bruce, one of Woody's assistant coaches [and later Hayes' successor]. And he asked me if I ever thought of going to Ohio State," Plank says. "And I say to him, 'Coach, that's the *only* place I *ever* wanted to go.'"

He says it's a decision he'll never second-guess. The complete experience, even if he didn't play regularly until his senior season, was loaded with opportunities.

"I didn't appreciate what Ohio State was all about until I'm there running out of that tunnel to the bench across the field, and, I mean, your feet never hit the ground. It was like an out-of-body experience," Plank says. "I'm telling you, it was Woody. He injected so much enthusiasm into everything there. The atmosphere [in Ohio Stadium] was part of that."

Hayes' command of nearly everything left Plank and his teammates often in awe of their coach. "We knew he was a legend. Just to be there was something," Plank says. "Early in the week in the locker room, there would be the usual chatter and talk. By Wednesday, things quieted down a little bit. By Thursday, we were ready to tear the doors off the locker room. Friday? Saturday? Forget it. From Thursday on, it was game time.

"Woody didn't very often use football in his talks to us. He referred to us as a team of leaders and a multinational force, a combination of the best from everywhere. Nobody could paint the picture like Woody could.

"You know," Plank says, "I am so fortunate to have played for this man. My success in pro football with the Bears and in business—and in life—just wouldn't have been had it not been for Woody."

* * *

Greg Lashutka, the former mayor of Columbus, credits Woody Hayes with having an indirect link to saving his life.

Lashutka, an Ohio State cocaptain his senior season in 1965, suffered a heart attack in the early spring of 1997. To clear artery blockage, Lashutka underwent an angioplasty, whose development was guided by three Ohio State medical school graduates. One of the developers of this particular procedure, Dr. Don Unverferth, was a former OSU football player under Hayes.

"The late Don Unverferth, Charlie Bush at OSU, and J. B. Simpson, my former roommate who's now in San Francisco, are proof that the Old Man touches people in different ways," Lashutka says.

Hayes' insistence that nothing was more important than one's education led many former Buckeyes to pursue careers in the medical and legal professions, among others. Lashutka says Unverferth and the angioplasty are the perfect embodiment of that. The coach's preachings and teachings spurred Unverferth, Arnie Chonko, Lashutka, and others into a professional setting where they could help make their world a better place.

Woody was always teaching his players, and it wasn't always about football, a grateful Lashutka says.

"I fondly remember those Thursdays in the Bell Tower," Lashutka says. "Woody's legacy was not wins and losses; it was the lessons he taught us in the tower. History. Everyone, whether they liked it or not, got a 'minor' in history from Woody, because life is history and we learned a lot about both from the man. Woody was a lover of the meaning of life, and that's history.

"I remember that we sat there and heard about Rommel, World War II, Greek-Roman traditions, Patton, Eisenhower. It gave a sense of greater purpose to the game than that it was just a game. It taught us that if we play as a team we win, and if we play individually we lose. It was all part of the fact that he cared passionately about each one of us."

After Lashutka had finished his tour of duty with the Buffalo Bills, he was nearing the end of another with the U.S. Navy. He remembers bobbing in San Francisco Bay, deciding which way his life was going to turn. Lashutka says he was leaning toward going back to school for his master's [of business administration], but in a phone call with Hayes was convinced otherwise. Convincingly. "He said, basically, 'You're going to law school,'" Lashutka says. "It worked out well for me. He cared equally as much about us, or more, after our playing days. I revere the man."

As students of history, player and coach had a rare occasion to be guests in a history class taught by Rhea Foster Dulles, the brother of former U.S. secretary of state John Foster Dulles and a noted author. Actually, Lashutka was the student and Hayes was his guest.

"He was a lover of history, and I was a history guy, so I invited Woody to come to class with me and listen to Rhea lecture. So Woody came down, and I came down, and Rhea wondered, 'Who is the son of a bitch who invited Woody to my class?' Well, I was the son of a bitch. The faculty did not roll over for the guy."

Lashutka says Hayes felt as at-home at the Faculty Club as he did on a football field. "There wasn't anything he couldn't discuss with the professors," he says, "but he didn't talk much about football with them."

Still, Hayes was successful as a coach, Lashutka believes, because he "had a strong sense of purpose, because he looked at the world by way of analogy, because 'scholar-athlete' meant a lot to him and because hard work could overcome a lot.

"Woody had a strong sense of leadership and a passion for it. He was a helluva guy. He didn't really care what people thought of him, but he loved his players, the university, and his family. If the public misunderstood him, so be it."

His motivational techniques might have left some scratching their heads, but Lashutka says he and his teammates knew better when all was said and done.

"One summer during practice, it was terribly hot, maybe in the nineties," Lashutka remembers. "In the middle of practice, he blew his whistle and we gathered around him. And he started to tell us about Duffy Daugherty, who was then the coach at Michigan State.

"He told us how Duffy would bring his team together [in a similar setting] and give them these ice-cold Coca-Colas. He said that was a sorrowful thing to do, then told us to get back to practice. . . . And 10 minutes later, a Coke truck pulls up to the practice field! He had a sense of humor."

Lashutka's coach should be remembered a number of ways, he believes.

"History should remember Woody Hayes not as a coach, but as a molder of people, players, and family," Lashutka says. "He was a coach's coach, a man's man, and a teacher's teacher."

* * *

The Woody Hayes that Tom Marendt remembers was an unpre-
dictable man. "That stands out the most with me," Marendt says,
"because he could have a one-megaton blowup one time, yet be
thoughtfully intelligent and perceptive another."

Marendt, who played defensive end for the Buckeyes in 1971 and
1972 and now works in grassroots government in the Indianapolis
area, says perhaps the perfect example of how one never could read
Hayes came on the occasion of a team meeting the coach called.

"It was a general meeting during summer ball, and no one, not even
the assistants, knew what it was about. We were all bugging the
coaches, and they'd just say, 'We don't know!'" Marendt says.

"So we go in and sit down, and Woody starts a lecture on products,
specifically telling us why we must buy American products."

Hayes, as the players sat quietly—looking at one another as if to
ask, "What's this all about?"—railed on against the preponderance of
imports and lamented what it meant for the American worker.

"He specifically singled out the Japanese and Germans," Marendt
recalls. "I don't think at the time that imports had the market share that
they had perhaps in the early eighties or maybe now, but it certainly
raised concern with the economists. And Woody.

"And the more he talked about it, the more agitated he became. He
said, 'We beat the Germans and the Japs [in World War II], and now
we're buying *their* products!' No one knew what to say, but one assistant coach, I really can't remember which one, was sitting near me, and
he cracked, 'Does that mean I can't buy Scotch anymore?'

"Not once in this speech did Woody mention football. Not one ref-
erence. He kept going on about how our market was being flooded by
foreign products and how we had to do our part [to stem the flow]. He
gave us some background on the war, and he talked about sacrifices. I
can remember so vividly [that] he got so angry about the Japanese
more so than the Germans, because we had too many players with
German heritage."

So crafty was Woody Hayes that he often got the best of his opponents, leaving them with revenge on their minds. Photo courtesy of Ohio State University Sports Information Department.

Marendt remembers the gathering as a study in stunned silence. Later, when the meeting was over and the players began to talk amongst themselves, Marendt says the general consensus was, "Oh, my God. Woody has just lost it."

Yet, there were other, far more intense occasions when Hayes made it seem as if it were just another day, just another situation. Says Marendt, "Especially before games or at halftime, he was generally very calm. He huddled very quietly with his assistants, talking, I expect, about what we were going to do next, plotting his strategy. And his pregame speeches bordered mostly on, 'Be aggressive. Be hard-nosed. Get after them.' He always figured that was the manly way to get things accomplished."

Marendt says he believes Hayes perceived himself as a military sort because he was absorbed by everything military. "In World War II, he might not have exchanged fire, though it was no fault of his own. But he didn't get to participate the way he wanted to; he was in charge of a ship. Maybe that's where the aggression came from."

Marendt's pensive tone turns to near-hysterical laughter as he begins to reveal another side of his coach. "During the season back then, Ohio State always had an open date. If other schools played ten games, we played nine, and we always played one or two games before the students came back to campus in the fall," Marendt says.

"Anyway, one year after the second game, we had our open date. And so Woody, believing he was being generous, called us together after the game and said, 'OK, no meetings this weekend. I expect you back Sunday at 11:00 P.M.' Keep in mind, he was telling us this at about 4:00 in the afternoon, the day before we had to be back! We were like, 'Hey, thanks a lot, Coach.' And then he tells us about how when he was a commander in the Pacific he always told his men he didn't want them coming back from shore leave with [venereal disease] and he said the same thing to us! He said he had run the cleanest ship in the Navy, that his had the lowest rate of VD, and he didn't want it on his football team!"

Yes, that was Marendt's Woody. But so was the man who Marendt characterized as hell-bent for education, very bright and funny while at the same time being extremely human. "We all learned some very basic fundamental values from Woody," Marendt says.

One of them, however, was not the way he conducted himself in hotel foyers when the team was playing an away game. It was during those times, he says, that one could observe the coach at his most focused best.

"Everywhere we went, everyone hated Ohio State," Marendt says. "So when we got to our hotel, Woody really would just barge right into the place, walking with a purpose and maybe a chip on his shoulder. And the people there would either shudder or scramble to get out of his way. Had someone there said, 'Can I help you?' he probably would have been like a little lamb. But it was always us against them, and, 'You'd better tighten your belts, because we're coming after you.'"

And now, after so many years away from the experience, Marendt says he finds his memories of his days under Hayes centering mostly on the coach's personality, organization, generosity, and preparedness. "I was able to learn that Saturday afternoons, like so many things in life, were a product of something else. Playing for Woody and being around him was a great experience, and I wouldn't give back any of it."

* * *

Woody Hayes called John Hicks the greatest offensive lineman he ever coached. Hicks, a tackle, was the driving force behind the vaunted Buckeye running attack from 1970 to 1973. And playing that role for Hayes, Hicks says, was easy.

"He loved his players and he was intensely loyal to them. And work ethic . . . he had a tremendous work ethic," says Hicks, now a commercial real estate specialist in Columbus. "He always said, 'I'm not very pretty, and I can't sing, but I can outwork them.' It was a very simple approach. I do it myself today. It's very simple. You just outwork everybody."

Hicks and his teammates were so far superior to almost every opponent that it seemed as if there were far more competition during practices at the old North Facility. The lofty status enjoyed by the Buckeyes might have had some teams strutting, but not Ohio State. Hayes didn't permit it.

"He beat the shit out of me at practice," Hicks says. "Well . . . not really, but he did slap me around a little. He didn't want you to get a fat head. You have to remember that [when he was a starter] we finished 19–2–1."

It almost would have been excusable for Hicks to get a fat head. He nearly pulled off in 1973 what certainly would have been the greatest accomplishment in college football history; he won the Outland Trophy and the Lombardi Award and finished second in balloting for the Heisman Trophy.

Hicks, a two-time All-American, says the Buckeyes succeeded because of their belief in the man who coached them. "He set such high goals for himself, and he expected the same of you. And let me tell you, he really had a way to bring you down to earth.

"He threw me out during a practice scrimmage. Really, he put the 'fix' on with the refs—we always had referees at our scrimmages—and all of a sudden I hear, 'We got a hold here.' And then here comes Woody, and he says to me, 'You're our right tackle and you just cost us a touchdown in the national championship game!'"

Hicks says he believes Hayes was highly accomplished because he took "a process and made it very simple. And that's the way he lived his life. It might seem corny, but he stood for country and flag. He didn't live large, he didn't have a membership to Scioto Country Club, and he certainly didn't need the press."

Hicks, who was inducted into the College Football Hall of Fame in 2002, wants Hayes to be remembered as someone who gave so much to those around him. "A lot of people who were in his life are a lot better off today. He simply made people better, and you can put football aside. It was his commitment to life, period."

* * *

"You just have to think of him at this time of year," says Randy Hart, fresh off the practice field one early spring evening at the University of Washington.

Hart, who played on the offensive line for the Buckeyes from 1969 to 1971, is careful to comport himself as Woody Hayes did on the practice fields at Ohio State years before.

"He'd just put his face into the wind, with no jacket on, and continue on," Hart says. "He wouldn't allow himself or his assistants to put their hands in their pockets, either. One time, he caught an assistant doing that, and instead of saying anything to the coach, he had the equipment manager sew all the pockets on the coach's pants shut. I guess the coach found out the next day."

Hart, assistant head coach for the Huskies, may be somewhat of a throwback to his former coach's era, but he says he doubts Hayes would get along well in today's athletic climate.

"He'd be mystified," Hart says. "It's a different game now. Back when he was coaching it was enough for most guys to play for the love of the game. Most of that is gone now, and I don't think coach Hayes could handle that if he were here."

But the Hayes that Hart remembers was tremendously personal, taking special care to really get to know not only his superstars but also the end-of-the-bench crew.

"He was way ahead of his time," Hart says, "tremendously interested in education. It carries over, too. Now you couldn't be a Woody Hayes or Joe Paterno guy and not be interested in education. Shoot, for three consecutive years, the top three students in the Ohio State med school were all former players of Woody's."

It was Hayes' insistence on attaining one's degree that helped lead Hart to the belief that he, too, one day should teach. He had settled on getting his master's degree in education, which would have allowed him to teach and coach.

"I told him what I wanted to do," Hart remembers. "He said, 'No, you have to go to law school.' And I said, 'But, Coach, I want to teach.' And he said, 'Oh, go on. If you ended up with a [law degree], they'd probably promote you out of the classroom anyway.'"

Hart says Hayes was the consummate salesman on many fronts, chiefly with respect to recruiting.

"He was prepared, unbelievably prepared. He wasn't a bullshitter," Hart recalls. "He covered all his bases. I was easy for him. I was just a fish. When I was on my recruiting visit to Ohio State [which, along with scores of other schools, was vying for Hart's commitment], Woody called me into his office. And he asked me why I wouldn't want to come to Ohio State. I couldn't answer.

"He suggested we just shake on it. I couldn't right then, either. And then he said, 'I've met your parents. How about we just give them a call?' Son of a gun if he didn't have my number right there on his desk next to the phone."

The next thing Hart knew, Hayes was dialing the Hart household in Willoughby, Ohio.

"And so he says, 'This is coach Hayes, and Randy is here and I think he'd like to be a Buckeye, but he wanted to consult with you first.' So I get on the phone, and my dad is on the other end. And he says, 'He got you, huh?' And I said, 'Yup.' And that was that. I was so totally enamored of the guy. I don't think I would ever have not gone to Ohio State."

Hart remembers Hayes as a great role model and a good person. "He always would want the best for his players, his coaches, and his former players and coaches, sincerely and honestly."

It was, at times, hard to believe when one was under Hayes' watch, Hart says. "It was always, 'Push them now. Later, they'll understand.' Even the guys who didn't really like him—some despised him—still understood. And you know what, unless they left for somewhere else, they always got their education. Woody made sure of it."

What Hart has wondered about since his days on the banks of the Olentangy is whether Hayes set up his ouster from Ohio State after the 1978 Gator Bowl.

"He had such deep respect for military heroes, guys like Patton and MacArthur. Those guys were dismissed, relieved of their command. I've often thought that it might've been possible that coach Hayes went out the same way."

One day approximately six years later, shortly before Hayes' death, Hart had lunch with his former coach. "It was at about the time when he wasn't seeing very well," Hart says. "I drove him to his house and helped him up the stairs to the door. I think to myself, 'This is the same guy who tormented the shit out of you.' Then he says to me, 'Randy, I need you to help me get the key into the lock; I don't see very well anymore.'"

At that point, Hart turned comedian. He says now, chuckling with growing intensity, "Coach, there are a lot of guys who would want to be standing at the top of the stairs right now with you."

No, Hart never pushed. He pulled instead. He says he pulled in every granule of wisdom he could from the coach. "What I learned

Woody Hayes and some of the "fellas" get together for a postpractice chat in the early fifties. Photo courtesy of Ohio State University Sports Information Department.

from coach Hayes was basically this: be a good person, and help others as much as you can. And work. If you're rich? Work. If you're poor? Work. If you're as successful as you think you can be? Work harder."

Hart also says he tries to treat his players the way Hayes treated him. Respect is key, he says. "I remember I did something wrong in practice, and he absolutely chewed me out, right in front of the whole team. And I was pissed. I mean, hot!" Hart says. "But Woody never wanted you to go to bed being upset. So, he'd find you somehow.

"I had gone to eat dinner, and Woody came up to me and said, 'Randy, you don't feel very good right now, do you?' And I said, 'No, sir.' And he said, 'If that [mistake] costs us the Michigan game, the Rose Bowl, and the national championship, you'd feel worse than you do right now, right?' Well, he'd gotten me again. It was his way of making amends."

Hart tells the story, probably as defining as any, of Hayes when he was hospitalized and visited by Hart and Glen Mason, the head coach at the University of Minnesota and former Buckeye lineman under Hayes.

"Here he was, supposedly recuperating, and we walk into his room—and he didn't know we were coming—and instead of laying back in bed as he was supposed to, he was fully dressed in his suit and tie, with shined shoes, his face shaven, his hair combed, sitting on the edge of his bed. The man had so much pride and toughness, he wasn't about to let *anybody* see him in a hospital gown."

And then Hart zeroes in on how to best characterize Hayes.

"He was a chameleon," Hart says. "And that's why he was so successful at everything he did. He could adapt to anything."

* * *

Carm Cozza got to experience the early coaching days of Woody Hayes. He was a standout player on Hayes' final team at Miami University in Oxford, Ohio, in 1950.

"It's a shame people didn't get a chance to see Woody from both sides," says Cozza, who retired as Yale University coach in 1996. "It was hell all week long, but it was wonderful on the weekend because he was so well organized and such a competitive person."

Impressive words, considering the source. Cozza spent 32 years as the head football coach of the Elis. He retired with 179 career victories.

"I remember one time I had a [physical education] class at 8:00 in the morning. We came in, and there was Woody in his office, and the film was going around. He hadn't gotten an early start; he had been there all night."

Cozza also remembers how tough Hayes was—to everyone. "We were going on a trip and his son [Steve] was going along. He was just a youngster, but Woody wouldn't let him on the bus since he didn't have on a tie. Our captain took off his tie and slipped it out the window to the youngster so he could get on the bus. Boy, he was tough. He would make us run the same play 30 times in a row. He'd almost tell the opponents what we were going to do and say, 'Try to stop us.'"

Cozza says Hayes was a stickler for education, whether in the classroom or on the field. "He was tough on anyone who misused the English language. He'd stop practice to correct your language, but in the next breath, he'd be swearing at you," Cozza recalls. "It was almost like your father doing it. He'd kick you in the butt, but you expected it. I used to kid him that I thought my name was 'You SOB' until I was a senior. He had a way of getting into your face. When he laughed, I laughed. When he cried, I cried. And when he got mad, I just hid."

Years later, Hayes invited Cozza to the OSU spring game.

"I was sitting in the stands, and he was on the field coaching both teams. He got upset at something that happened on the field. He yanked off his glasses, broke them, and cut his hand. A poor manager was trying to put a towel around Woody's hand to stop the bleeding, and he kept flapping his hand at the manager. Finally, he hit the kid— not hard—and flipped him over the bench. The people in the stands were hysterical."

Cozza did get an assist once from Hayes in the recruiting wars.

"Woody and I were both recruiting a great quarterback out of Cleveland St. Ignatius by the name of Brian Dowling. Woody felt he was losing him, so he had the governor call him, and he sent a Valentine to his mother. Woody was a tremendous recruiter. In the home, there was no one better. He called me and said, 'I'm concerned if you don't get him, the kid might go to Michigan.' Woody could accept a recruit not going to Ohio State, as long as the player didn't go to Michigan. That's how competitive he was."

Cozza recalls with sadness the last time he saw Hayes alive.

"Right before he died, Miami honored our Salad Bowl team from 1950. He was very ill, and the doctor wouldn't let him go. Woody told the doctor, 'I'm going! You can come with me if you want, but I'm going to be with my boys!' They drove Woody down in a limo. He showed the game film and got on each of us like he would have 40 years before. . . . They took a picture. . . . He said good-bye. . . . That's the last time any of us saw him.

"He was something special . . . just special."

* * *

Don Sutherin was a sure-footed kicker for the Buckeyes from 1955 to 1957. His 34-yard field goal provided the winning points in OSU's 10–7 Rose Bowl victory against the University of Oregon in 1957. The victory gave the Buckeyes the national championship.

Forty years later, what Sutherin, then the head coach of the Hamilton Tiger-Cats of the Canadian Football League, most remembers about his days in Columbus and his time with Hayes was the Old Coach's recruiting job.

"Woody had my brother and me down to Columbus from Toronto, Ohio. We had lunch at, I think, the Olentangy Club," Sutherin recalls. "And he asks, 'You like shrimp?' And of course I said I did. Farm boy that I was, I dug right in, and I ate the shrimp—shells and all. Woody never could get over that. He laughed. He let me do it! And he kidded me about it for a long time."

Sutherin, whose father died when Don was 14 years old, says Hayes was a father figure to him. "He was always caring, and he always wanted the best for you. But sometimes, you'd get mad," he says. "As tough as he was on the field, he was very generous off it."

And most of that generosity, Sutherin remembers, revolved around one of Hayes' beloved pursuits, "and it didn't have anything to do with football. Education was the utmost, first thing to Woody. Football came second. He always made sure we had study tables and that we were at them, and tutors, too. He was graduating most of his players right up to the end."

Ask Sutherin why Hayes was and still is considered a legend in the coaching profession, and he'll tell you the answer is rather simple.

"He had such a desire to succeed. It overshadowed everything in his life," Sutherin says. "Even Anne—what a wonderful lady!—was second to football. He lived and studied the game so completely, and his assistant coaches were very, very solid people."

Another chuckle summoned by a memory of Hayes also dealt with gastronomic pursuits, if not the pursuit of a certain player from Toronto, Ohio.

"When he and [assistant coach] Gene Fekete came to recruit me, Woody ate a pie and a half of pumpkin pie," Sutherin recalls. "He didn't recruit me! He recruited my mother! He always went after the parents. And my mom said I was going to OSU."

For Sutherin, though, it wasn't always a bed of California roses. "I had a situation that was more my fault than anybody's after my junior year," he says. "I had trouble in class, and Woody didn't like that. He took my captain's job and gave it to Leo Brown. Although I couldn't blame Woody, that devastated me."

Sutherin quickly forgave and forgot that tough time, and when he got into pro football coaching he used to spend a lot of time chatting with Hayes about the nuances of the game. He credits Hayes for helping him to become a successful coach in the land where you get three downs to make 10 yards and the field is 110 yards long.

"He was a hard worker and a stickler for detail," Sutherin says, adding just like Hayes, "if I was paid by the hour [as a coach], I'd be a rich man by now!"

* * *

In the hills high above Tempe, Arizona, sits a monastery. It is an edifice about which Woody Hayes had a bunch of questions. That's how Jimmy Moore remembers his coach.

Moore, only the second Arizonan recruited by Hayes, played for the Buckeyes from 1975 through 1978 as a tight end, going on to a pro career with the Baltimore Colts as an offensive lineman. But he achieved nothing before answering all of Hayes' queries.

"He came to recruit me on my birthday, January 28," Moore remembers. "I played basketball for my high school, and he came and watched me. And then we had to take him up into the hills. He asked me a lot of questions about it. He wanted to know everything."

His thirst for knowledge quenched, Hayes turned his attention toward Moore's mom and dad.

"My mom, she had heard bad things about Woody. She was skeptical. My dad figured how bad could it be if all these parents were sending their kids to play for Woody," Moore says. "After Woody left, my mom had my bags packed!"

The meeting between Hayes and the Moores began a relationship that exists today. Anne Hayes and Jimmy's mom still talk by phone a couple times a year. Moore says the two women developed a friendship during his freshman season at Ohio State.

"I got my knee hurt against Illinois that season, and then I got sick when I was in the hospital," Moore says. "Mrs. Hayes came up to my hospital room every day, just like she was my mother. She knew I liked red pop, so she used to bring me some every time she came up. And she'd get my mom on the phone and tell her there was no need for my parents to come to Columbus, that I'd be home in a month and that she'd look after me. Which she did."

Moore said Anne Hayes' phone calls to Tempe were made nightly throughout his hospitalization. Looking back on the whole Ohio State/Woody Hayes experience, he likens it to a tremendously gratifying sense of family. He always knew Woody was committed to him, and he was committed to Woody. But what Anne did for Jimmy and his family, he says, was above and beyond what anyone would expect.

"I think many coaches lack a sense of family now," Moore says. "It wasn't like that when I played for Woody."

Moore readily acknowledges he was "Woody's boy." He used to get teased about it, but it was a lofty perch from which he would not be budged.

"I *was* 'Woody's boy' and I'm proud to say I was," Moore says. "He never made any secret that I was a favorite of his. It didn't bother me."

Certainly not at the training table, anyway.

"We used to go to the Ohio State golf course [restaurant] before home games, and we'd all pig out on the pecan rolls; they were the best! Well, one night Woody raised hell because we were eating too much. And the next week, he had all the linemen sit with him at dinner. When the rolls came around, he picked the pecans off his and gave them to me. Everyone kind of stared at me. I ate them all! See? 'Woody's boy.'"

Not every day was like *Father Knows Best*, though.

"He got on me a couple of times, and good!" Moore exclaims. "I missed a block in practice, and [two-time Heisman Trophy winner] Archie Griffin was carrying the ball and just got smacked. And that's when Woody goes off. 'Do you want to get this guy hurt?' He's screaming this in front of the team. I'm embarrassed at this point. He chewed me out."

It's never too late, or the wrong time, for a little more coaching. Photo courtesy of Ohio State University Sports Information Department.

But Moore says his coach "never really got on me that much." Others? Of course.

"I saw it all the time," he says. "I knew he cared about his players, though. It was not malicious. It was like my dad said: 'How bad can it be?' But he would scream and holler and tear his T-shirts and break his glasses."

Moore breaks into a great baritone chuckle.

"You know, he called me into his office one day and we were talking about something, and he realized his desk drawer was open," Moore recalls. "He slammed it shut. Really quickly, I mean. I saw what was in that drawer! He must've had 20 pairs of eyeglasses in that drawer! You know, the ones he was always breaking when he got mad? He liked to play those psychological games. Boz [equipment manager and coconspirator John Bozick] used to cut Woody's T-shirts so they'd be easy to tear if he got angry. And the back of his hats, too!"

Moore says Hayes was a great coach not because of Xs and Os— "We were three yards and a cloud of dust, not the Dallas Cowboys"— but because he was a motivator.

"He made you work harder," Moore says. "He would work you so hard and take you to the point where you'd feel like you were going to die, and then he'd give you some water."

The last time Moore saw Hayes was shortly before the coach's death.

"It's kind of sad, but they were having a Woody Hayes roast at the Aladdin Shrine Temple," Moore recalls. "I had gone to his office in the ROTC building and he asked me, 'Do you know anyone who wants to come to my party?' It was like he knew he was going to die. He kept asking and saying, 'I'll pay for them if they can't afford it. They have to be there.' And for the next hour and a half, he made calls. He was inviting everyone he could think of, telling them he'd pay their way. He just wanted everyone together again, one more time.

"I'm sure he knew he was going to die. It was so sad."

Moore says he and all the other former players and coaches who attended the roast had a photo taken with Hayes. He says he wants a copy of that photo more than anything but has not been able to track it down.

But Moore, has other mementos from his time with Woody.

"When he was fired, he went to his office and took away only the things he wanted," Moore remembers. "And later some of us went in there, after he had cleaned out, and took the leftovers. I opened one of his desk drawers and lifted a piece of cardboard. There were 10 to 15 checks in there from 1961, 1962. He had never cashed them. They were all from speaking engagements. One hundred, two hundred dollars. Uncashed checks. I'm hanging on to them."

Moore summarizes his coach as a man he'll always remember for being "very caring, demanding, passionate, and a guy who loved what he did."

* * *

As a football coach, Woody Hayes had to be the most dedicated.

That's how former Ohio State All-America linebacker Randy Gradishar, a member of the College Football Hall of Fame and a retired All-Pro, 10-year veteran with the Denver Broncos, characterizes the coach for whom he played from 1971 to 1973.

"He went beyond 100 percent to do whatever he could do for his players," Gradishar says. "There was never a question that the coach didn't know what he was doing."

Hayes carefully cultivated relationships with his players, Gradishar says. "It's just that I didn't realize it until I became older. He was very sincere, and he modeled that to his coaches. 'I want you to get to know these kids,' he'd say to his coaches. So the position coaches would [among other things] have picnics for us. But Woody was always there. He always challenged you. Especially on the academic and scholastic side. He was a great example. Guys like Joe Paterno are successful because they put extra time into getting to know you."

Gradishar and his coach became close. "Woody was like a second father to me," Gradishar says. "I love my dad, but I never had any kind of relationship with him because he was always working."

Hayes knew what he was getting when he signed the lanky kid from Champion (Ohio) High School.

"When he came up to recruit me, he asked to see my dad, who owns a grocery store," Gradishar recalls. "Woody says, 'Let's go.' So we got in the car and went down to the store. Woody studied families, mostly the parents, as much as if not more than the kids. He wanted to see what kind of family structure there was."

Indeed, Hayes said time and again that the home to which one was tied was as important as the accomplishments a prospect had accumulated. He looked for discipline, commitment, love, trust, and honor. In the Gradishar household, he found it.

When he got to Ohio State, Gradishar expected the strict discipline. "He would keep on your case and tell you to do better," Gradishar says. "He got more out of his guys than they thought they had to give. . . . It gets back to his perspective, his focus."

And that included intensity. Gradishar remembers preparing for an OSU–Michigan game.

"It was a Monday or a Tuesday and we had this team meeting," he says. "And he was strategizing in military terms on how we were going to attack Michigan. Then it got silent. The next thing you know, he throws the water jug into the chalkboard. I remember thinking, 'What the heck does that have to do with Michigan?' But it sure caught everyone's attention."

Gradishar says there was no visible or audible reaction to this, one of Hayes' patented megaton blasts. "We probably weren't allowed to gasp," he says. "Everyone probably went into internal shock."

Gradishar, the father of two daughters and a son, lives in Denver. He tries to apply to his work the very principles that made Hayes a leader in his profession. He ticks them off, rapid-fire: "The preparation, the willingness, being a people person, the knowledge, the philosophy. He got the talent to get first downs, beat Michigan, win the Big Ten, and go to the Rose Bowl."

He says people are sadly mistaken if they assess Hayes as nothing more than a hard-nosed coach. "He had people skills," Gradishar says.

Randy Gradishar, a standout linebacker for Ohio State in the seventies, adamantly refutes those who claim Woody Hayes had no people skills. Photo courtesy of Ohio State University Sports Information Department.

"Any successful coach had people skills. The public perceived Woody as a tyrant, but that was how he was portrayed in the media. He always did what was the right thing for his team.

"Modern-day people, or those of this era, will remember him for hitting that kid from Clemson. You always remember that last moment; it's the critical spirit we have as human beings."

Gradishar characterizes Hayes as one who was totally committed to his university, Columbus, college football, and his players and staff.

"And I really respected him for the way he spoke his mind," he says. "I'm learning to do that now. Right or wrong wasn't the issue. I remember feeling, 'Man I'd like to be like Woody.' He was so honest about what he thought and felt. He had my respect. I'd like to be more like that."

The last time he saw his former mentor was in the mid-eighties in Columbus.

"I felt that I needed to go back and share my Christian faith with him," Gradishar remembers. "It was a real step in my personal life. Here I am, 35 or 36 years old, and I'm going to talk to my coach. I invited him to go out to dinner . . . and throughout that conversation, I took the lead [which rarely happened in any conversation with Hayes], and I told him about my personal faith journey.

"I told him, 'The greatest decision I ever made was when I accepted Christ into my life.' He acknowledged that, to what extent I don't know. I got no response. Maybe he didn't know how to or want to. It was very rare for him not to respond. But I can honestly say he respected that, because if he disagrees, he tells you. There was not a lot of conversation after that."

Through it all, Gradishar says he "loved the guy for the good and the bad, because of the impact he had on my life."

* * *

As an All–Big Ten end who played for Ohio State from 1952 to 1954, Dean Dugger was privy to a wide array of situations involving Woody Hayes. One of them, said Dugger, helped to drive home just how intense the coach could be.

"I remember one incident in preseason practice where we were running a play and kept messing up," said Dugger, who died in 2000 while awaiting a heart transplant. "So Woody had us run that play 10 times. The first time, we didn't do it right.

"'Do it again!'

"The next time, the same thing.

"'Do it again, damn it!'

"By the fifth time, he was clenching his jaw and his face turned red. By the seventh or eighth time, he was down on all fours in the middle of the huddle screaming, 'Shit! Shit! Shit! Shit! Now, goddamn it, get up here and do it right!' The ninth or tenth time we finally got it right. He had tremendous intensity."

Dugger said he indirectly might have been the benefactor of Hayes' philanthropy. "He made it possible for one of my sons to get into law school, I believe," Dugger recalled. "My son was delayed in graduating from Ohio University because he had cancer. Woody stepped in and got him enrolled in courses at Ohio State so he could finish his degree, and I'm convinced, although we have no proof, he later helped my son get into law school at Ohio State."

And so Dugger preferred to talk more about Hayes the man than Hayes the football coach. That's the kind of impression he left on Dugger.

"We, the disciples, knew the man, not the coach," Dugger said. "He was so committed to education, and at the time you didn't realize it but he was always pushing and pushing you to bring out the best in you. He knew the abilities and the potential of his men, and he knew how to bring it out."

When it came to football, Dugger remembered Hayes as a man who constantly was giving it his all. "He worked harder than anybody. And he would work you hard. There were times where, sure, you wanted to challenge him, but I never did.

"Sure, if he was wrong, he'd admit it. But he would remain very adamant about things until an assistant [coach] would mention something like, 'Woody, that's not right.' And Woody would say, 'OK, let's try it your way.'"

The influence Hayes had over him really didn't strike Dugger until he was long gone from campus. "It was much greater after I left college," Dugger said. "A few years later, you began to realize the strength of character in the man. You know, I lost my father when I was 14, and I always had strong coaches. That firmness [of Hayes] I really expected. And now as I look back, I continue to develop a greater admiration for him."

Dugger also characterized Hayes as a humble man, "probably because of what his players could do. But he never took the credit. He was the most principled man I have ever met. He had strong beliefs and wouldn't deviate. And there were not many coaches who could sit down for lunch at the Faculty Club and . . . talk shop. Not football, but the academic world."

Dugger, in summary, said he remembered Hayes "as the hardest-working man, who respected people, would not pass judgment on people, and who had a strong, strong belief in his university and in education. That was Woody Hayes to me."

Chapter Two

The Assistants

Earle Bruce, Lou Holtz, Ara Parseghian,

Bill Mallory, George Hill, Larry Kindbom

"You couldn't possibly be around coach Hayes without him having a profound influence upon your life."

—former University of Notre Dame football coach Lou Holtz

Earle Bruce had the fortune (misfortune?) of succeeding Woody Hayes after Hayes was fired in the wake of the Gator Bowl incident. But Bruce's hiring almost didn't transpire, and it had nothing to do with the interview process he went through in 1979. Nothing close. It had everything to do with an occurrence when Bruce was enrolled at Ohio State.

"I got injured during practice and I thought to myself, That's it. I thought it was over. I so badly wanted to be in that stadium and be a part of all that tradition," Bruce recalls. "But I decided to hitch home. I was out on [U.S.] 40, the old National Road, heading home. Woody found out about it, and he sent [assistant coach] Harry Strobel after me. He didn't catch me.

"When I got home, my mother said, 'Coach Strobel called and he wants you to call him.' So I did, and he said, 'Coach Hayes wants you to come back, help coach the team, and get your education.' I couldn't believe it!

"Of course, I went back to Columbus. And you know, I played for him or coached for him for six years. He was my mentor and was very influential in my deciding to become a [head] coach."

These days, Bruce divides his time between the coastal North Carolina town of Wilmington, where he and his wife, Jean, have a home, and Columbus, where he is coach and general manager of the Columbus Destroyers of the Arena Football League. When in Wilmington, he sneaks off to the beach or to play a little golf. He loves his life, and he loves the road he has traveled.

Bruce went from the assistant coaching job at OSU to high school positions at Ohio high schools in Mansfield, Salem, storied Massillon, back to Columbus as an assistant, off to the University of Tampa as the head coach, to the same position at Iowa State University (where, coincidentally, Hayes' older brother, Ike, had been an All-America football player decades before), to Columbus to succeed Hayes, to Colorado State University, to two Arena Football League jobs ("I loved that game!") to where he is today. Hayes played some sort of role in Bruce getting the job in almost every situation. Bruce claims, "A call from Woody Hayes was something that was very well received."

Bruce says working for Hayes was "like being in the Marine Corps. It was a great experience, but I'd never do it again," he adds with a laugh.

"Truthfully, I've never seen a man work harder than he would. He was very focused, tough and firm. And, as much as you might not know it, Woody Hayes was a people person. He really liked people. He wanted to know all about you. Oh, he could be very difficult at times, but he liked people."

Bruce and his fellow assistant coaches often were on edge, he says, never quite knowing exactly what to expect out of the Old Man, when they might be temporarily fired or given any number of odd tasks.

"I remember I had 'movie duty.' That meant I had to arrange for a movie the night before games. He picked the movie, though. I remember we were up at Minnesota and we saw *Easy Rider*. We had been averaging 47 points a game, but we didn't get it the next day [after the movie]. Coach Hayes asked, 'Who picked *Easy Rider*?' I said *he* had, but that I was in charge. He fired me from movie duty right there. Boy, was I relieved! I was so relieved it wasn't funny. I was happy to have someone else take over that job.

"And then I got the 'record job.' I knew nothing about music. So he walks into the locker room, and I hear, 'Oh, my God! Who's in charge of the music?' I lost that job, too, which I was relieved about. I'm just

Woody Hayes (back row, left) assembled a top-flight staff for the national championship run of 1968. Among the coaches: Earle Bruce (back row, fourth from left); Lou Holtz (front row, left); George Chaump (front row, second from left); Rudy Hubbard (front row, third from left); and Bill Mallory (front row, right). Photo courtesy of Ohio State University Sports Information Department.

glad I wasn't the quarterback coach. George Chaump got fired about 94 times. We were always getting fired from individual jobs!"

Bruce says he and his former colleagues tend to forget all that tension, because they remember Hayes more for his charisma, his intensity, and his commitment to his staff, his players, and the game of football.

"He had great tunnel vision," Bruce recalls. "And I think he was the greatest thespian on the practice field with all his carrying on."

Bruce says he believes Hayes enjoyed success because he and his staff worked diligently at recruiting and preparing for games.

"He was damned involved in it," Bruce says. "And he was tough. Guys like Woody Hayes put toughness in the game of football. He was tough on the field, gentle off it."

When Hayes was in command, Bruce says, there were no ruts. "That didn't happen at Ohio State University," he says. "There were too many good players, smart players, and a lot of fear and anxiety and wanting to do better."

Bruce says recruiting the right kind of player to Ohio State was tough detail, but the way by which it was done made it easy on everyone.

"Coach Hayes ran an absolutely clean program," Bruce says sternly. "Coach Hayes never set up anything shady. The good schools like Penn State, Notre Dame, Michigan, and Ohio State just don't cheat [today], and that's a tribute to coach Hayes."

What surprised Bruce about Hayes was his sense of vision. It's as if he were a seer.

"In 1966, he told the players, 'Every single one of you guys has to be prepared to use computers. You have to take computer class!' That was in 1966, for Pete's sake," Bruce says. "He was ahead of his time."

The Old Coach should be remembered, too, Bruce says, for the 28 years of service he gave OSU.

"He loved the university and education. He loved Ohio and the United States of America. And he loved football," Bruce says. "They were all tied together."

* * *

Lou Holtz, the head football coach at the University of South Carolina, was fired and rehired by Woody Hayes three times between January 1968 and July 1969. The rehirings usually came within minutes. To hear Holtz tell it, Woody, the son of a bitch, was always firing someone.

"I could tell you stories about the insane things he did," Holtz says, remembering how one of his duties as an assistant coach on Hayes' staff was being in charge of the practice field at Ohio State. "He called at 1:30 in the morning. We were supposed to get a little bit of rain, but the field was real hard and the groundsman felt we needed a little bit of water on it, so I made the decision not to put the tarp on the field.

"That 'little rain' turned into a monsoon. And, you get a call at 1:30 in the morning, wanting to know if the tarp was on. And you said, 'No,' and I mean . . . the next thing you know, he's got the whole staff out there putting the tarp on the field, ankle-deep in mud."

Fired. Gone. History.

"You talk about getting a chewing out. Hey, I've been in the service, but nobody could chew you out like coach Hayes. It's a warm memory now; it wasn't then," Holtz says.

The second "end" of Holtz's career at Ohio State was in December 1968. The official traveling party was at Pasadena preparing to meet the University of Southern California in the Rose Bowl on New Year's Day. Holtz and some others decided to head for Sunset Strip in Los Angeles for dinner and conversation. As he was leaving for the outing, he thought about his rooming-list and bed-check responsibilities.

"I had the rooming list not only for the players, but for when the players' wives came out," Holtz chuckles, recalling Hayes' penchant for organization. "You moved the players in with their wives. And then, so many days before the game, they moved back and the wives roomed together and the players roomed together. He had about nine different rooming lists, and I had bed check!

"We all went down to 77 Sunset Strip for dinner the day the wives got in and I was to be back for bed check at 12:00. Unfortunately, I had never been in California before and there was so much traffic on Sunset Strip," Holtz says, recalling the mess. "I'd never seen traffic like that. It was a zoo, and I got back late."

And guess what happened?

"I was fired. I mean, I was fired on the spot."

It was almost as if it were a precursor to the George Steinbrenner–Billy Martin relationship.

The third time? "That was probably for a justifiable reason," Holtz says sheepishly. "It was out on the practice field. When we got to spring practice [in 1968], they had great athletes on offense—[Rex] Kern and all those guys. But we had some on defense—[Jim] Stillwagon, Jack Tatum and Mike Sensibaugh, [Mike] Polaski, [Ted]

Never one to closet his emotions, Woody Hayes makes his point during a game in Ohio Stadium in the seventies. Photo courtesy of Chance Brockway.

Provost, [Doug] Adams, Tim Anderson. When we would get involved going against one another, it was like we [the defense] were Michigan.

"And he got upset because we had some good athletes that could do some different things. He got really mad—and Kern was behind him, and Kern started laughing when he was chewing me out. And I started laughing. I wasn't laughing at coach Hayes, but he thought I was. No, I was laughing because Kern was laughing. And it was just one of those situations."

So long. It has been a pleasure knowing you.

Holtz says his memories of Hayes are warm. Chief among those recollections is the effect Hayes had on those who worked or played for him.

"You couldn't possibly be around coach Hayes without him having a profound influence upon your life," Holtz says.

There were times when the going got incredibly tough. So much so, in fact, that Holtz says, "At one time, you would absolutely want to strangle him."

But everything in a relationship with Woody Hayes had an equalizer, and for every contemplated "strangling" there was always another element to send the scale plummeting in the other direction.

"Yes, there were other times where you admired him, you always respected him, but after you left him you truly loved him," Holtz says.

And the reasons for that are many.

"I think coach Hayes was the most intelligent, wide-read individual that I have ever been associated with on a continuous basis. I mean, the guy was absolutely a very smart individual, read incessantly—and I'm not just talking about football. I'm talking about life and politics, chemistry, history. The thing that he impressed me with was, well, several things: number one, a very, very fundamental individual. His football team always blocked and tackled very well. He was very simple in his approach but with very, very high standards. He would set that standard.

"But then he wouldn't get rid of the people that didn't measure up to the standard; he would show you how to reach that standard. He worked with you. He had a tremendous compassion for his players. I mean, he genuinely cared about them as people."

The tenor of Holtz's voice deepens. He remembers the time in 1969 when the son of one of Hayes' former players died in an automobile accident. It happened as Hayes was conducting his cherished spring football practice. He believed spring practices were critical to his team's development, a chance to enhance skills and attributes for the fall. One minute he's there, coaching and chewing out players and assistants, the next minute he's gone.

"An individual's son was killed, inadvertently, and coach Hayes missed several days of spring practice to go down and be with that former player, because he thought that former player needed him," Holtz says, declining to name the player.

But Hayes' compassion didn't end with one episode. And it clearly transcended the lines of the football field. Holtz says it was not out of the ordinary for Hayes to spend countless hours tutoring his players—not on the Xs and Os of football, but on English, history, math, you name it. "He wanted them not only to be good football players, he genuinely cared. And he wouldn't accept a B if you were capable of getting an A. That was just a standard he had," Holtz says.

Holtz says as much as Hayes stood for excellence, he was a walking symbol of dedication. "He never went through East Liverpool, Ohio, after I coached for him, that he did not call my mother just to find out how she was.

"He would go to Vietnam, and I know this firsthand, and he would come back from Vietnam and spend his weekends calling various parents of people that he met to tell them he communicated with a son, and what messages the individual wished to send back. And he did this at his expense. I could go on and on and tell you about human interest stories. I could go on and tell you the tremendous things that he did as a football coach.

"Predominantly, he was a great teacher, set a high standard, and was fundamentally sound. . . . There's nobody I respect any more. He was just a super individual."

As much of an impact as Hayes had on Holtz the person, the same holds for Holtz the football coach. After he left Ohio State in 1969, Holtz took the head coaching position at the College of William and Mary. From there, he moved to the top jobs at North Carolina State University, the New York Jets, the University of Arkansas, the University of Minnesota, and the University of Notre Dame. And Hayes always was there for his protégé.

"No doubt about it. For years after, if I had a problem—even up to the month he died, and I don't think I'm different than any of the other coaches—if I needed some advice, I'd always call him. If I had a big decision to make, I called him," Holtz says.

Success. Hayes oozed success. And folks like Lou Holtz soaked it up. Holtz has been a terrific success at almost every stop in his career, and it perhaps culminated with the 1988 national championship for Notre Dame.

For Holtz, it all goes back to one man.

"I think that coach Hayes was very successful because he just refused to accept anything other than success," Holtz says. "He believed in Ohio State. Whatever Woody did, he was totally committed to it. There was no fringe area with coach Hayes. When it came to defending Ohio State University and selling it, I mean [he did so] at all costs. If it came to football, if it came to academics, whatever coach Hayes did, he just got thoroughly engrossed in it and had the unique ability to get everybody around him as engrossed and as interested in what was happening as he was. . . . Boy, when he made up his mind to do something, he did it completely. Hours meant nothing. That's number one in why he was so successful."

Holtz says that's why, to this day, Hayes is revered by those he touched. And he had considerable contact with thousands of people from 1951 to 1978 at Ohio State.

"I've never talked to anybody who played or coached for him that didn't absolutely love him after they left. Nobody," Holtz says firmly.

But when you were in the middle of one of Hayes' legendary megaton blasts, or were on hand as he launched into a protracted session of nit-picking, Holtz said it was sometimes difficult to see the positives.

"But I want to tell you something: I learned to coach exactly as coach Hayes taught me. And everybody does the same thing. But, boy, I'll tell you what—and I firmly believe this—as long as there are the philosophies of the Bo Schembechlers, the Earle Bruces, the Bill Mallorys, coach Hayes will always live. Because, there's no doubt, we all learned to coach just like Woody Hayes taught us."

Holtz says so much of what the public saw, heard from, and read of Hayes was accurate. But it was incomplete. He says he's sorry the public didn't get the opportunity to experience Hayes' other side.

"If your only association with coach Hayes was through the news media, I'm sure your remembrances of him will not always be exactly the same [as those of people who knew him well]. I don't condone everything that coach Hayes did by any stretch of the imagination, but I can understand.

"I do love him and I do respect him, and if you didn't play or coach for him he ought to be remembered as an individual who made this world a better place. And although you may not have agreed with everything, he was successful—whether you're talking about winning football games, transforming people's lives, or caring about those that aren't quite as fortunate."

* * *

For Ara Parseghian, it all began with a hip injury he suffered as a member of the Cleveland Browns in 1949.

Woody Hayes, then the coach of Miami University, got wind of Parseghian's misfortune and offered the injured player a chance to be a graduate assistant coach on Hayes' staff at the Oxford, Ohio, campus. Parseghian, who was working on his master's degree at the time, jumped at the chance and joined Miami for the 1950 season. Eventually, Parseghian would succeed Hayes at "The Cradle of Coaches," the school that sent Hayes, Parseghian, Bo Schembechler, John Pont, and others on to bigger schools and into the limelight.

Parseghian talks about Hayes as if he were still alive. His initial recollection: "The man is 98 percent good and 2 percent explosive, and, unfortunately, he explodes 98 percent of the time in public. What the public viewed, unfortunately, was the public part," Parseghian says.

He should know. In teaming with play-by-play announcer Keith Jackson on ABC-TV's telecast of the 1978 Gator Bowl in Jacksonville, Florida, Parseghian witnessed, firsthand, Hayes' worst moment. With the game on the line and Ohio State seemingly driving for the go-ahead touchdown against Clemson University, quarterback Art Schlichter's pass was intercepted by Clemson middle guard Charlie Bauman. What happened next depends on where you sit: either Bauman taunted the Ohio State sideline by waving the intercepted ball in the Buckeyes' faces or he was celebrating the most important play of the game. Regardless, Hayes fairly flipped his lid, slugging

90

The national championship team of 1968 was proof of Woody Hayes' recruiting prowess. Photo courtesy of Ohio State University Sports Information Department.

the Clemson middle guard and later, it appeared, his own offensive lineman, Ken Fritz, who applied a bear hug to his out-of-control coach. Woody was fuming. Clemson won the game, on Hayes' darkest night, 17–15.

The next day, Hayes was gone. Fired. His career with the Buckeyes was over.

But Parseghian says Hayes shouldn't be remembered for his ill temper, although Parseghian confirms it truly existed. Instead, the former University of Notre Dame and Northwestern University coach wants Hayes not necessarily canonized but respected for his recruiting methods and emphasis on clean play.

"You should have seen the relationships that existed in his recruiting endeavors. He became a friend to all," Parseghian recalls. "He preached education and honesty. He spent countless hours recruiting cleanly and overcoming, honorably, the other guys.

"His relationship with parents was more grandfather than father figure to the kid he was trying to recruit. And when you saw these things, you realized he was going after more than just an outstanding athlete; he was going to make this kid a man."

Just as Hayes was a portrait of cleanliness in the living rooms of America, Parseghian says Hayes wanted his team to be just as immaculate in its play on the field. He was extremely intolerant of penalties committed during a game by his players.

Parseghian says, "Avoidance of penalties was critical! From a technical or strategic standpoint, he had an obsession with the elimination of penalties. That rubbed off on me as a coach. He always said more penalties didn't necessarily make a team tougher. Avoiding them did."

As for the Hayes image, Parseghian put it at the feet of the media—although he acknowledged it was Hayes who freely chose to lose a wheel occasionally in press conferences. He would rebut, often vociferously, the views of writers and broadcasters. And, in the end, that stamped Hayes with varying labels, some of which were none too complimentary.

Shedding his insurance executive and coaching fronts, Parseghian turns almost nostalgic in summing up Hayes.

"He did so many good things, because deep down inside he was a very, very good person."

* * *

It's fairly simple, if you ask former Indiana University coach Bill Mallory, a one-time assistant to Woody at Ohio State, what stands out about Hayes.

"His commitment to the game of football," Mallory says. "He put a great deal of commitment into it, and I can tell you no one worked any harder. When I think about commitment and coaching, the first person I think about is Woody."

As he did with his players, Hayes often counseled his assistant coaches on a variety of matters, especially education. Mallory was no exception.

"I was with Woody for three years, and then I went to Miami of Ohio," Mallory remembers. "Woody said he wanted to talk to me before I left. So I went to see him, and he said to me, 'Remember what's number one with these young men. Education. See that they get that education.' I followed a lot of those guidelines, and it wasn't lip service from Woody. His feeling was, get an education and graduate . . . and be well prepared."

As a coach at practice, Mallory found Hayes to be continually stressing soundness, underscoring how vital it was to every facet of the program. "There was no way he was going to beat himself," Mallory says, "and that was a trademark of Woody's teams. There were a lot of reps in practice, and he was great in preparing for the big one."

As a person, Mallory found Hayes to be far less intense. "He was very caring," he says. "Woody was particularly caring and compassionate when people were in need. If you needed help, Woody would be there. I know this, he always bent over backwards for me. Compassion, a lot of compassion."

Mallory saw a part of the humorous side of the Old Coach, too. "Every time my wife [Ellie] was pregnant, we went to a bowl game," Mallory says, chuckling at the recollection. "Well, in 1968, my wife was pregnant. And I told Woody about it, and I said, 'You know, that's going to be in our favor. We'll go to a bowl game.' Well, he lit up like a neon sign. He said, 'I'll tell you right now, that makes me feel good.' And then he kept calling to check on Ellie, asking if she was feeling OK, things like that. And we did go to the Rose Bowl that year and won the national championship."

Mallory, who was in coaching for 40 years, says Hayes was one of the best because of what he stood for. "He had a fantastic record. He wouldn't take a backseat to anybody. His teams were well coached and he was dedicated to the profession.

"He was just an outstanding individual. He cared about people making something of themselves, and his players were good, productive individuals."

* * *

George Hill was an assistant coach for Woody Hayes for eight seasons, from 1971 to 1978, and considers Hayes a great man. But like everyone who worked for Hayes that long, he didn't avoid Woody's wrath.

"Probably the worst butt-chewing I ever got from Woody—and I mean he reamed me up one side and down the other—was because one of my players flunked an English test," says Hill, formerly an assistant coach with the Miami Dolphins. "He climbed all over me. 'If we lose this guy, it could cost us a Big Ten championship, because we can't afford to have this player ineligible. Hell, you're an English major. You should have been tutoring him and made damn sure he got that test done.' He ripped me for 15 or 20 minutes about as hard as you can get ripped.

"Well, the next day I was in my office, and Woody walked by. I thought, 'Oh, boy, I hope he's over that.' He walked in, sat down, and handed me a cup of coffee. 'You take your coffee black, don't you?' he asked. We talked for a while, and he was trying to let me know that he still loved me and thought I was a heckuva guy. Once Woody chewed you out about something, it was over. You didn't hear about it again. I guarantee you, he got my attention. The rest of the quarter, I did tutor that player in English. The kid ended up getting a B in the class."

Hill says there was nothing phony about Hayes' emphasis on education. "He didn't do it because it was fashionable. He believed that the only way the university could repay the players for the time and effort they put into the program was to graduate and get a degree. He had us tutor astronomy, physics, all kinds of subjects on the freshman level. This was before they had the brain coaches or study tables. We did it whenever we weren't out on the road recruiting. It was just something that Woody expected."

Although Hill says Hayes was never paranoid about what to expect from an upcoming foe, there was one time when he did show a trace of apprehension. It was Hill's first season as an OSU aide and the week of the Michigan game.

"Michigan had a great football team, and we were not that good that year. We had played pretty good defensively, but offensively we were struggling a little, because we had lost all our players from the year before through graduation or injuries. I was asleep, and at 1:00 in the morning on the Wednesday before the game, I got a phone call. It was Woody.

"'My God, George, I've been over here looking at these pictures'—
he always called films pictures—'how in the hell are we going to stop
that backfield of [Ed] Shuttlesworth, Billy Taylor, and [Glenn] Doughty
and that bunch? That's the greatest backfield I've ever seen. How the
hell can we do it, George?'

"I was half asleep, but I told him, 'Coach, I've faced a lot better
backfield than that.' He snapped back, 'What do you mean, you've
faced a better backfield than that?' I said, 'Yeah, last season when I was
at Duke, coaching against you, I had to find a way to stop Brockington,
Zelina, Hayden, and Kern. That was a helluva lot better backfield than
Michigan's is.' He said, 'You're goddamn right it was. We'll be all right
then, won't we?' And he hung up."

* * *

It was the summer of 1977, and Larry Kindbom was moving to
Columbus.

"I had been at Kalamazoo College and Western Michigan University and was looking around for places to work on my Ph.D. I had
played football and done some coaching, but I was always a small-
college guy. I didn't have a sense about what major college football was
about. I was just looking to help out the football team some way and
thought all I needed to do was make a call and offer to help."

Kindbom was driving from Michigan when his truck broke down in
Sandusky, Ohio. He had some time to kill, so he took the opportunity
to call the Ohio State football office to make his first contact and schedule an appointment.

"I called from a small restaurant and was told by coach Hayes'
secretary that Woody would be able to call me back in a few
minutes."

When that designated time came, another patron was using the
restaurant's phone. Kindbom, now the successful head football coach
at Washington University in St. Louis, explained to the person that the
football coach at Ohio State would be calling him there any minute.

That was Kindbom's first indication that Hayes was more than just another football coach.

"When the guy got off the phone, he announced to everyone in the place that Woody Hayes was going to be calling the restaurant. Fortunately, when the phone rang, it was coach Hayes. Everyone at the restaurant crowded around me to hear my conversation. I had no idea why they were so interested."

Kindbom set up a meeting and then got his truck fixed. When he arrived at St. John Arena, Hayes' secretary informed Kindbom that the coach was extremely busy and wouldn't be available right away. As Kindbom was explaining to the secretary that he was on a tight schedule, Hayes overheard him.

"He came right out and introduced himself. I told him I was interested in helping out the team—handling the towels, anything. He then started asking me about my background. I told him that after I graduated from college, I thought about attending law school. I had been accepted to a number of schools but had been turned down by my home state school, the University of Michigan, so I figured maybe I wasn't cut out for the law.

"Without saying anything, coach Hayes got on the phone and called the dean of the Ohio State law school and began telling him about me. He was trying to get me enrolled in the law school!"

Kindbom tried to explain to Hayes that he no longer was interested in attending law school and had other educational aspirations in mind, but Hayes shushed him. Finally, Kindbom concluded that Hayes "had lost all his marbles."

"I told him I had other appointments and was running late, so I waved good-bye and headed out of the office while he still was trying to get me into the law school. I didn't get to the end of the hall before he came out of his office and asked me to meet him for breakfast."

Kindbom met Hayes the next morning, and the conversation eventually turned to football. But not until Kindbom had become intrigued and entranced by Hayes.

Hayes' trips to Vietnam were self-financed. His mission: to raise the troops' spirits and let them know that he and the folks back in the States cared. Photo courtesy of Ohio State University Sports Information Department.

"He gave me a ride back to campus in his flatbed truck, and I honestly thought that was the last time I would see him. I was walking away and was halfway across the parking lot when he yelled at me to come to his office the next morning."

Kindbom was there as Hayes arrived. He followed the head coach into a staff meeting with the assistant coaches. Once inside, Hayes wasted no time in introducing Kindbom as the new "volunteer assistant in charge of the wide receivers."

Says Kindbom, "That was news to me. I glanced around the room at the assistant coaches, and they all looked a bit surprised. After the meeting, the coaches wondered how I got the job. The one in charge of recruiting graduate assistant coaches showed me a file of 300 résumés, some from full-time assistants at major colleges trying to get on the Ohio State staff any way possible. When I told them my story, they couldn't believe it."

Kindbom spent two years at Ohio State. "I hit it off with coach Hayes from the start. I was usually one of the first ones in the office, so we had a lot of time to talk. We talked about a lot of things, including football. I learned a great deal in those two years."

Today Kindbom heads one of the strongest small-school programs in the nation. Something rubbed off in his tenure at OSU.

"Woody was a tremendous individual who believed you win with people. He was an educator who ran the program like a small college. I don't know if I even would have stayed in coaching if I hadn't met him."

Chapter Three

The Staff and Administrators

Chris Boadt, Chance Brockway, Larry Romanoff, John Bozick,

Jim Jones, Harold Schecter, Ed Weaver, Rick Bay,

Marv Homan, Al Hueve, Richard Armitage

"We worked hard and were very demanding of our kids academically. I don't know how his ideas would go with today's youngsters."

—former OSU athletic director Jim Jones, Hayes' first "brain coach"

Chris Boadt was a student intern in Ohio State president Ed Jennings' office in 1985. One day he was approached with an assignment: "We need someone to drive Woody Hayes to his physical therapy sessions every day for the next two weeks," he says he was told.

"Who is Woody Hayes?" Boadt asked.

"I knew zero about football," Boadt says now. "I really didn't know the impact of it. I thought it was no big deal. I just pick up some old man at his house and take him for treatment. Before I got the position, coach Hayes wanted to approve me. I was a 19-year-old, smart-alecky kid, so I was hoping I'd pass the 'test.' I went to the hospital to meet him. He was in bed, and his son, Steve, was in the room with him. I told him, 'Coach, there are a couple of things you ought to know about me. The first thing is I don't know anything about football, and I've never been interested in football. You also should know that my dad graduated from Michigan, my mom from Michigan State, and I was born in Michigan. And I don't really understand why you don't like Michigan.'

"He looked over to his son and shook his head, then looked up at me and said, 'I'll teach you everything you need to know to love football. And the Michigan stuff, people make too much of it. Bo Schembechler is my best friend.'"

Boadt got the job. When his two weeks were up, Hayes asked Jennings for Boadt to continue the help. Boadt was a fixture around Hayes for the next two years.

"One of the things I did was take coach Hayes to the home football games. He had a seat in the press box. The first week he was having difficulty seeing what was happening on the field, so he asked me to explain what was going on. He soon realized I didn't know what I was talking about. I said, 'The guy in red, he ran down and the guys in white tried to get him, and he ran across a line and the guy dressed like a zebra raised his arms.'

"After that, we got Woody a big TV monitor and [*Columbus Dispatch* sports editor] Paul Hornung started to sit with us to explain what was happening."

Boadt used his own car—"an old beat-up, rusted-out Subaru in need of a new muffler"—as well as a Chevrolet El Camino Hayes' former players had given him as a present years before.

"Coach Hayes was invited to a lot of very nice functions, and many times I'd pick him up in my old car. He didn't care. He was very low key and didn't want anything fancy. He was truly a down-to-earth person.

"There was one time when he was invited by Jack Nicklaus to attend the Memorial Golf Tournament at Muirfield Village. He was going to ride around the course in a cart following Nicklaus and President Gerald Ford. He got a special parking permit so we could park right in front of the clubhouse. So there we are in my Subaru, driving through all these checkpoints on the way to the clubhouse. None of the security people could believe I had a pass until they saw coach Hayes in the passenger seat. I pulled up to the front door and there are Mercedes, Porsches, limos. I drive up and a valet comes out. The door on the passenger side sometimes stuck, so the valet had a tough time opening it. I told the valet that I'd prefer to park the car myself. I pulled it around to the side so as not to embarrass anyone."

Boadt says Hayes wasn't concerned about luxuries or publicity. "I got to know who Woody Hayes really was when we went to the cabin his former players helped build. It had one electric line and no telephone. There was enough power for only one or two lights. I went with him a couple of times and he'd just sit there and think. He was

Among the many outstanding assistants who served on Woody Hayes' Ohio State staffs was one Glenn E. "Bo" Schembechler (front row, second from left). Photo courtesy of Ohio State University Sports Information Department.

very private and valued his solitude and the time to think and work on things that were important to him."

Boadt says he is indebted to Hayes for teaching him the importance of punctuality. "He always said, 'If someone takes the time to set up an event, whether it is in your honor or you're just an invited guest, you need to have enough respect to show up on time.' If the event was scheduled for 6:00, we weren't there at 5:55 or 6:05, but exactly 6:00. We always left early for the event, and I can't tell you how many times we popped into a Wendy's for a cheeseburger and a Diet Coke . . . and we waited until [it was time to] go to the event. His wife, Anne, usually packed a bag lunch for him. Coach Hayes was a diabetic, so there would be carrots, an apple, and a little sandwich. She also would include his insulin. I had to learn to give him shots, so I had to do that on occasion, too."

Boadt vividly remembers a trip to one event, a reunion of coaches at Miami University in Oxford, Ohio. "We arrived way ahead of schedule—as usual—so he asked me to drive around for a while. We drove around the university and then he told me to take a road out into the country. We wound up on a road in the middle of a farm. He told me to take a dirt road into the middle of a cornfield under a huge oak tree. We parked under the tree. He asked me to get out of the car and give him some quiet time to himself. I stood out in the middle of a cornfield for 15 minutes, but I figured, 'OK, he's the boss.' I went back to the car and shared the lunch that Anne had packed. He then explained to me that when he was coaching at Miami, that was the place where he went before every game. He spent time under that tree thinking and collecting his thoughts. It was an absolutely beautiful and peaceful setting. He said he hadn't been there since he was coaching at Miami. He wanted to go back and think about his times there."

Boadt says he would have worked for Hayes forever. But when Woody died, Boadt was forced to make a decision. "I would not call myself a stellar student. I had devoted all of my time to coach Hayes, because he became such an important person in my life. He was always on me about studying. He always impressed upon me what a great change the military had made in his life. He introduced me to a lot of people from the Navy and the ROTC, so I wound up going into the military for three years."

Today Boadt—minus his trusty Subaru—is in Las Vegas, working in the Nevada attorney general's office. "After coach Hayes passed away, Anne gave me the El Camino. When I went into the military, I gave it back to her. It was auctioned off for a fund-raiser. I learned a lot in that car. Coach Hayes was an example of how to be a great human being and an example of how people should treat other people . . . but I still don't know much about football!"

* * *

Chance Brockway began documenting Ohio State athletic contests in 1956. He was designated the "official" team photographer, so he was able to obtain an inside look at Buckeye sports.

"I shot all of Woody's home games from 1956 through the end of his career," said Brockway. "A lot of people seem to think I talked with Woody, and they don't believe me when I tell them I never had a real conversation with him. I only saw him at the ball games. He was busy with his job, coaching, and I was busy taking pictures."

Brockway had more than 500 shots of the coach, but some of them clearly stood out. "I took one of him in a white shirt throwing something on the ground. That's the most published photo of him I have.

One of photographer Chance Brockway's favorite photos of Woody Hayes—and an odd sight at that. Photo courtesy of Chance Brockway.

That's probably been in 20 books or magazines. I also have a color shot of Woody and Bo [Schembechler] that I took out on the middle of the field in 1976. I generally sell 30 or 40 big prints of that every year around Christmas. But one of my favorites is a sequence of Woody out on the field arguing with an official. Woody finally was being escorted to the sideline by the official, and Woody's got his arm around the ref's shoulder. They look like old buddies."

Brockway claimed that Hayes was among the most photogenic coaches of all time. "Some coaches are terribly hard to get a picture of because they are never animated. They always have the same look on their face. Woody, from a photographer's standpoint, had quite an ego. He liked to have his picture taken. Hell, he'd stand there on press day until you ran out of film. He was always putting on a show."

* * *

Larry Romanoff enrolled at Ohio State in 1969 and worked as a student manager for the football team. He joined the athletic department as an academic counselor following his graduation. In 1991, he was promoted to assistant athletic director and later was responsible for the school's National Collegiate Athletic Association compliance services program.

He said he was lucky to still be working for the university, considering the number of times he was "fired" by Woody Hayes.

"As academic counselor, I did all the grades for football and helped the players with their class schedules. There was always a lot of pressure with Woody, because he was such a perfectionist. One quarter we had 105 guys on the football team. I got the grades that quarter and we had only one guy who didn't have above a 2.0 grade average. For football, that was an excellent, excellent quarter. I was extremely proud of myself. I was finally going to get an 'Attaboy, Larry!'

"I was putting all the grades down on a sheet. For Woody, I had to organize it in a very specific manner. He wanted the seniors first, juniors second, and so on so he could tell what the hours meant. He didn't want it alphabetically. I got it all neat, exactly like he wanted it. I was in my office at 6:00 in the morning. He always got in about 6:30, and I was all ready. I heard him coming down the hall humming to himself. He saw my door open, came in and asked, 'Larry, what are you doing here?' I said, 'Coach, I've got the grades.' I was smirking a little, because I knew I had him. He couldn't get mad at me over anything. He sat down and started looking through the grades and he found the one guy. He looked at me and threw the papers on the floor as hard as he could and jumped out of the chair. He tried to rip the papers with his feet by jumping on them. He walked over to my file cabinet and kicked in the side of it. I had a three-tiered in-box and he started pounding it until it looked like a *V*. He turned to me, told me I was fired, and stormed out of the room. Here I am, shattered. I thought I had done one of the best jobs in the history of Ohio State academics and I got fired. Later that morning, he went to the coaches' meeting and I wasn't there. He told the guys, 'We had a real good quarter, but don't tell Larry about it, because he'll get a fat head.'"

As a student, Romanoff worked his way up to the role of head football manager, but it was his first experience with Hayes that was most memorable.

"I was a freshman and the freshmen usually just worked with the freshman coach and players. A lot of the older managers were sick one day, so I was told to work with the varsity. I was assigned to coach Hayes. There was a drill called the half-line drill. You took slip-overs and marked so many yards to one side and 17 yards to the other side so the backs knew where they would be running out of bounds from the hash mark. I got the balls there and had all the slip-overs and asked the freshman [team] coach, John Mummey, if I needed to mark the lines. He said, 'No, you don't do that!' So I'm standing there watching the drill and the first back runs out and there's no line marked. Coach Hayes starts blowing his whistle and yells, 'Where's my goddamn manager?!' Where's the goddamn manager?!' He turns around and I'm standing right behind him with all the slip-overs in my arms. He looked at me and yelled, 'You dumb son of a bitch!' and started whacking me on the shoulders with both hands. This was my first day with the varsity and he's hitting me! He said, 'Get those things over there and mark that line!' I looked over at coach Mummey and he just turned around and walked away."

Romanoff credited Hayes with instilling life-lasting work habits in all his aides.

"Coach Hayes was a perfectionist. He wanted all of us to work harder than everybody else. We learned to come in early and stay late. He made sure we knew everything about every player. I could recite the class schedule and location of every kid's classes every quarter. That's what he expected, not just from me, but from all the coaches on the staff."

* * *

John Bozick was the equipment manager for the Ohio State athletic department for more than 30 years. During that time, he developed a close relationship with Woody Hayes that extended far beyond the field. Bozick said that wasn't unique on the staff, and there was a reason for that.

"The only word, is C-A-R-E. He cared. That was Woody's greatest asset. He had his temper, but he cared about you—not only the kids, but the whole staff. We worked as a unit, and he expected that. It was never I, I, I; just we, we, we.

"He surrounded himself with all kinds of personalities, and I think that's why we had such an outstanding unit. We had all kinds of people going in different directions, instead of everybody having to do everything the exact same way. He always respected other people's opinions and wanted to hear those different views."

Bozick often got credit for assisting Hayes in staged tantrums. The coach, trying to motivate his team in practice, would wait for a player's miscue, then jerk off his trademark black baseball cap. In a "show" of anger, he would rip the cap in half and stomp it to smithereens. Insiders say Hayes had Bozick cut the rim of the cap to make it easier to split, but the equipment man adamantly denied any involvement.

"That's not true. That's just not true. None of them was ever cut. In the old days, every baseball cap was very, very susceptible to being torn, so consequently, he could tear them. As time went on and we switched caps, he'd step on them and jump on them a bit, because he couldn't tear them apart. I don't give a damn how strong you are, you couldn't tear those apart. But I guess it made for a good story."

When Bozick spoke of Hayes, he did so with reverence.

"He was very colorful. He was a very expressive person. At one moment he'd do something, and the next moment he'd do something else. *Bang!* You didn't know what to expect. I knew the man, and he was a legend. How many times in a lifetime does anyone ever get to meet a legend, work with him, and have a close relationship? I'm just thankful I had that opportunity."

* * *

Jim Jones is remembered most as being the athletic director at Ohio State from 1988 to 1994. But if it hadn't been for Woody Hayes, he never would have been on track for that position.

"I was Woody's first 'brain coach,' as he called it. I also was the assistant freshman coach. I was at Ohio State to get a Ph.D. and was teaching a class in the physical education department when a friend asked me if I was interested in interviewing with Woody Hayes. I don't know any young person who ever played or coached in Ohio who wouldn't jump at that chance.

"Two or three weeks later, he called me at dinner time. I went over and we had a chat. He asked me various questions, like, 'Who was your best professor and why?' About a month later he called me back and wanted to hire me. I found out afterward that he had called all the people I had talked to him about. That was his way of checking references without asking for them."

Team physician Robert "Dr. Bob" Murphy always kept a close watch over the games and over his patient, coach Woody Hayes. Photo courtesy of Chance Brockway.

Jones said Hayes never blamed him for student-athletes' deficiencies. "He always blamed himself. That was the military in him. He felt that if he gave clear enough orders, the job would get done. All of us screw up, but coach Hayes never pointed out that you were involved. It was never directed at any individual."

But that didn't keep Hayes from steering Jones in the right direction. "In a staff meeting, coach Hayes asked me if I read for pleasure. I said, 'Yes, I do.' Then he threw this book across the big conference table at me and said, 'Here, read this. We have a quarterback [Rex Kern] taking psychology who needs to pass that class.' It was the Psych 101 textbook. [Kern] passed the class, needless to say.

"We had a very old-fashioned program that probably wouldn't work today, I suppose. There were a helluva lot of values in it. We felt like we knew more about getting an education than the freshmen did, so their lives were very structured and demanding. He had me send every freshman a book on vocabulary during the summer. They were required to come to camp with the book completed. Woody felt that helped them with their English classes. We tutored everybody as a freshman. We had a mandatory study table which you could earn your way off, or on. It was only required for freshmen and selected upper-classmen who he felt were not paying the price academically."

Education was very important to Hayes, said Jones. "He was a product of an educator father who ended up being a superintendent of schools who he highly respected. Coach Hayes prided himself in being a teacher. He wasn't a phys-ed major, so he came up through the teaching ranks. He felt like we could get the football out of our players in practice, but the most important part was that they got an education. He believed that we were giving them an opportunity and if they didn't get their degree, we were cheating them badly. We worked hard and were very demanding of our kids academically. I don't know how his ideas would go with today's youngsters."

Jones claimed today's players who leave school early for professional football would have driven Hayes crazy.

"I remember one former player, who shall remain anonymous, who was on the national championship team [of 1968]. He shook my hand at Ohio Stadium during one of Woody's memorial services. He told me it was the first time he had been back in the stadium since he had left school. I asked him why. He said, 'I was afraid to come back, because I knew coach Hayes would ask me why I hadn't gotten my degree yet.' That's the way he was."

Jones said we all have negative facets, but Hayes' positive side far outweighed his negative persona.

"I remember the time when Vic Janowicz was playing in the pros and was injured in an automobile accident. We were playing at Northwestern, and Woody brought him back on the team plane and had him taken care of at the University Hospital.

"I don't know anyone who loved this university more than Woody Hayes, probably to the detriment of his family. He never took a vacation, except to go to Vietnam to entertain the troops. Other than that, it was Ohio State University and football."

*   *   *

Each school in the Big Ten Conference is required to have a faculty representative. That person has a say in conference matters that pertain to academics as well as athletics. In most cases the designee is hand-picked by the university's president or athletic director because of his or her fierce loyalty to the athletic department.

Harold Schecter held the title of faculty representative for Ohio State from 1977 to 1983. He admitted being staunchly loyal to the university, but he always tried to be fair to the school's students and staff, rather than just rubber-stamp whatever the athletic department deemed necessary. He dealt with Hayes on many occasions.

"I have a remarkable story," said Schecter. "When I was on the university's athletic council, I also was a professor of chemistry. Woody and I were very good friends and had a tremendous respect for each other. At that time, Ohio State was only going to the four major bowls—Rose, Orange, Sugar, and Cotton. That restriction was coming up for a vote following the 1978 regular season, and Woody learned that I was very much opposed to going to the 'minor' bowl games. Since I was also the faculty representative, he knew that I had a fair amount of influence on the council."

A few days before the vote, Schecter got a call from Hayes. "I was grading midterms with a number of graduate assistants in organic chemistry, and he said that he had heard that I was opposed to Ohio State playing Clemson in the Gator Bowl. I told him that I knew Clemson was in trouble with the NCAA, and it was going to take action against them. I felt Ohio State should not be playing Clemson under those circumstances. His answer to me was, 'Well, you've prejudged this. They are not guilty until they are proven guilty and action has been taken. Therefore, I cannot accept that argument.' I said, 'The second matter in all this is that I don't think you have a good football team. You lost to Alabama in last year's Sugar Bowl and there were many of us who were concerned about how you responded to that. You were extremely concerned about that loss and a number of us talked about that.' His answer was, 'We football coaches are improving. We don't have a really outstanding team, but we're getting better and better and my coaches think we have a good chance of winning.'"

Woody then asked if there were any other reasons. "I told him, 'Woody, I think I know you very, very well. I don't think you will be able to handle this if you lose to Clemson. We were very concerned how you responded after the Alabama game, and I'm concerned how you will take it.' I was very frank with him and said, 'After having coached this long, people are saying you're getting old, and I don't think you can handle a loss.'"

The council did approve the Buckeyes for the 1978 Gator Bowl.

"I was sitting with the president of the university, but because of the fog and crowd on the sidelines, we didn't see [Hayes hit Clemson middle guard Charlie Bauman]. Those of you watching on television could see the incident, but we didn't know anything had happened. We got on the bus after the game and went back to the hotel. The following morning I went to the airport to go to the Rose Bowl. It wasn't until I was changing planes in Atlanta that I ran into someone from the Big Ten who told me that Woody had lost his job." Schecter had no idea he was prophetic.

"Woody went into hibernation for two months. No one saw him. He was invited to give a speech in Iowa. His brother was a veterinarian there. His introductory remarks were, 'I'm glad to be here, but I want you all to know that I wish I had listened to my good friend, Professor Schecter of the chemistry department.'"

A few years later, Hollywood producers were interested in doing a feature film on the life of Hayes. Woody asked Schecter to oversee the preliminary discussions. "I spent about two weeks with the producer and writer. Finally, we determined that the movie would be very popular in Franklin County and Columbus, Ohio, but there was no way it would have national appeal. Why? Because there wasn't a damn bit of sex in it!"

And Anne Hayes' reaction to that?

"She agreed with me completely!"

* * *

Ed Weaver was athletic director at Ohio State from 1971 to 1977. Ask him, and Weaver would tell you that Hayes was a model employee.

"It's hard to beat a winner, and Woody was a winner. He was a great football coach and had a great following. Nobody worked any harder than Woody Hayes. He was in the students' dormitories at night to make sure they were studying, and you never beat Woody recruiting if he could get to the family. In my seven years as athletic director, he took teams to the Rose Bowl five times.

"We all were on one-year contracts—the president of the university, Woody, the assistant coaches, me. I stopped into the coaches' meeting one morning and Woody said, 'We got our contracts today. You know something? I better send some of that money back.' He didn't know or care what he made. He never once negotiated a contract."

Weaver loved to recount his funniest experience with Hayes. "One year, Michigan State was being investigated by the NCAA. The sports editor of the Michigan State student newspaper wrote a story blaming Woody for turning the coaches in. The kid started calling Woody night and day. He called me night and day. He just wouldn't give up until one of us talked to him. He pursued the story so much, the Lansing and Detroit media picked up on the story, too. It became such a big deal that everyone connected with Michigan State was upset at Woody about it.

"We were scheduled to play up there that fall. Michigan State was providing us with extra security, but the morning of the game, I thought I better walk out on the field with Woody to give him some comfort. I didn't say anything to him, but as the team took the field for warm-ups, I fell in beside Woody. We entered the stadium, and by then there were already fifty or sixty thousand fans. We got out to about the goal line, and the noise started. We went another 10 yards up the field and it got louder, then got even worse. You've never heard such booing. By the time we got to the 30-yard line, you could feel the ground rumble. We got to the 35, and Woody was ready to go over to his offensive group. I looked over at him and you couldn't hear anything. He got a little grin on his face and said to me, 'These people up here don't like you much, do they?'"

* * *

Rick Bay had a unique perspective on Woody Hayes. Bay was part of the Ohio State–Michigan rivalry as a football player and wrestler for the Wolverines from 1961 to 1965. Later, he was the athletic director at OSU from 1984 to 1987.

Bay had two vivid memories of the border war. "My freshman season, 1961, I was a reserve quarterback, but since freshmen were ineligible at the time, I was in the stands in Ann Arbor. We weren't that good, but Ohio State had one of the top teams in the country. Late in the game, [OSU running back] Bob Ferguson scored his fourth touchdown of the game. They kicked the extra point and were ahead, 42–20. At that point, Woody took all his regulars out of the game. We ran a few plays and fumbled, giving the ball back to Ohio State with only a minute or so left in the game. Woody proceeded to put the starters back in, threw the ball on every down and scored a touchdown with only a couple of seconds left. To top it off, Woody went for two points on the conversion and made it, making the final score 50–20. I remember turning to the guy I was sitting with and [saying], 'I guess this really is a big rivalry!'"

115

The trademark Block O cap was as much a fixture on the sidelines as was the man who first made it fashionable. Photo courtesy of Chance Brockway.

Years later when Bay was the AD at OSU, he asked Woody about that incident. "His blood ran hot; he pounded the desk and yelled, 'That was a payback!' and cited some previous Michigan game that he felt the Wolverines had disgraced the Buckeyes in a similar manner."

Bay's second memory was his sophomore season, 1962, in the game at Columbus. "I was still a reserve quarterback and we were trailing, 28–0. It was late in the game and coach [Bump] Elliott was trying to get as many people in as he could. He finally called my name, and I was supposed to run a bootleg. I grabbed my helmet and ran onto the field, but before I could get to the huddle, the gun went off and the game was over. I didn't have any other chances to play in the rivalry."

When Bay went to work at OSU in 1984, he was concerned about how Hayes would receive the man from "that school up north."

"Woody got out of coaching in 1978 and was somewhat reclusive for a while, but by the time I got there, he was back on the scene and was the legend that he deserved to be. The university had established an office for him in the ROTC building. I was on campus for about a week, then made an appointment to go see him. I put out my hand and introduced myself, but before he would shake my hand he said, 'Young man, I have to tell you something. Nothing against you, but I wanted an Ohio State man for this job. Instead, we got a guy from that school up north and somebody from the football team. I can hardly believe it!' I said, 'Coach, if it'll make you feel any better, you can take out all the game tapes, look at all the clippings, and you'll see that I *never* did anything to hurt Ohio State football!' He got a kick out of that, laughed, and shook my hand. From that point forward, he was terrific."

Bay recalled getting awakened one cold March day in 1987 at 5:00 in the morning by a call from Dr. Robert Murphy, the team physician, with the news that Hayes had died.

"What I remember is most of the television media showed clips of the Gator Bowl incident. It saddened me that the incident sort of became his epitaph. He had done so many great things in his life, but the lasting memory was that one moment."

117

There was a private memorial service for the family and close friends at a Columbus church and a public service in Ohio Stadium attended by twenty-five thousand mourners. "At the church, Richard Nixon gave the eulogy. He was simply extraordinary. It touched everyone. At the stadium, the main speaker was Bo Schembechler. Bo was terrific, too."

Today the Woody Hayes Athletic Center sits on the edge of campus. Bay was in charge of raising $10 million for construction costs and oversaw the completion of the facility shortly after Hayes' death.

"We dedicated it with two games remaining in the 1987 football season, on a Friday. We were 5–3–1 and lost at home the next day to Iowa on the last play of the game. A day later Earle Bruce [Hayes' successor] was fired, and I resigned."

Bay surfaced as president of the New York Yankees, then became AD at San Diego State University.

"Looking back, everyone remembers Woody's tirades on the field, but what struck me was that I never met anybody who played for Woody who didn't cherish the experience. Couple that with all the work he did in the community as a volunteer that people never knew about and you have an extraordinary person."

* * *

Marv Homan served as the sports information director for Ohio State from 1973 to 1987 after training under veteran OSU publicist Wilbur Snypp. He also was the consummate gentleman, which sometimes made getting along with Woody Hayes a bit trying. But Homan preferred to remember the lighter side of Hayes.

"Woody was always a stickler for promptness," Homan said. "He had coaches' meetings virtually every morning, and the usual starting time was 8:00. One morning Woody was delayed a bit, and it was going to be close whether he was going to make his own meeting on time. To him, that was absolutely vital.

"I saw him in his car, driving through the parking lot faster than he should have been going. He was looking for a place to park, and the lot was pretty full. I imagine his blood pressure was going up, and he was pretty much steamed. He finally saw a space that he possibly could get a car into. He jammed his car in reverse and got it squared away and tried to get the car into the spot. He couldn't do it on the first try, but he was determined to use that spot. He put it in reverse again and got it perfectly square and slowly inched his way right into the space. He had to have rubbed the dust off the cars on both sides of him.

"Well, he opened the door, but there wasn't enough room for him to get out of the car. Now he was really steamed. He slammed the door shut, started the car, and backed it up. He put the car in neutral, got out, and *pushed* the car into the space. I guess he made the meeting on time after all."

Homan, always the publicist, used to have to bite his tongue to keep from spreading the goodwill Hayes was involved in. Woody didn't want attention focused on his hospital visits, small-town banquet talks, and late-night telephone calls to friends and unknown fans in need.

"There was such a good side of Woody, a warm side, that went unnoticed by many people on the outside. Even after a road game, despite the time, he'd go to the Children's or University hospitals and go in unannounced to greet some people. If they wanted to talk football, fine. If they wanted to talk politics, fine. He was an extremely good conversationalist. He did that time after time after time. The nurses used to comment on what a good therapeutic effect he had on people. Some of the patients didn't even know him, but by the time he left, they felt they knew him. He was a breath of fresh air. It was a way he felt he could do some good, and he did."

* * *

Al Hueve worked for Ohio State's athletic department, running sound equipment in its facilities. So, naturally, Al was on hand when Woody Hayes delivered the university's winter commencement address in St. John Arena in 1986.

119

"One thing that he told the graduates stuck with me and made me realize how much wisdom this man had," said Hueve. "Woody said this: 'Keep one thing in mind, no matter how good you think you are. There is probably someone who will outsmart you, and you can't control that. You have your given talents and limitations. But there is one thing that nobody other than you control, and that is how hard you work. Nobody can outwork you in your field of expertise unless you let them.'"

Hueve used that advice in his own career. "That philosophy is obviously a carryover from coaching, as Woody always got 110 percent from his players. When the chips are down in our department, I get to carry the ball a lot. My bosses know I won't quit, even if the tasks seem insurmountable. More often than not, I've proven the critics wrong."

Even though Woody directed his comments that day to the graduates, the others in attendance weren't ignoring his address. "A very sincere 'Thanks, Woody!' Your inspiration lives!"

* * *

A copy of Woody Hayes' book, *You Win with People*, bears a handwritten inscription: "To Dick Armitage: my friend, even if you didn't let us go to the Rose Bowl."

"It was 1961 and the Pac-8 was breaking up," said Richard Armitage, the former vice president of student affairs at Ohio State. "They reorganized and went to the Rose Bowl committee to start over. At that time everyone in the Big Ten was upset with our Rose Bowl deal. We never could get enough tickets. In addition, we had done a study of the athletes and they clearly said the season was too long. At the same time, the faculty at Ohio State felt that the university put too much emphasis on the importance of the football team instead of the importance of the academic programs.

"That fall, Ohio State won the Big Ten, but there still wasn't an agreement between the conference and the Rose Bowl. The Rose Bowl committee still invited Ohio State. The decision of whether or not to go went to the faculty council, which I was a member of. It voted 28 to 22 not to go. The students started a riot. Woody came and told the rioters to go home and they did. Minnesota ended up going to the Rose Bowl that year and eventually the Big Ten OK'd the contract with a number of reforms. But Woody never forgot it."

"Just after I moved to California, that's when Woody hit the opposing player [in the Gator Bowl in 1978]. I felt compelled to defend him. He was, number one, a coach who protected his players. He never, ever would say a negative word about a player. A player might end up on the third team, but he never put his players down publicly. He would always accept the responsibility and say that the coaching staff didn't do a very good job of coaching. I admired that, because his players came first. That word got around the state of Ohio, so he was able to get into the homes of virtually any recruit. Despite his violent temper, the parents of the players and the players themselves knew that Woody sincerely cared about them. He didn't pass that responsibility off to someone else. He was hands on, checking up on the students in the dormitory, in the classroom and at home in the summer. He also turned down some good football players who were marginal students. That pleased the faculty."

Armitage said Hayes also cared about the university. "He ate his lunch nearly every day in the Faculty Club. He would, and could, talk with history professors or anyone else there. The faculty admired him for his honesty and ethics. Woody would show up at the student government meetings and just sit there to listen to the agenda. He would be in the dormitories talking to students. He was truly interested about everything happening on campus."

Armitage pointed to two incidents that show Hayes' national notoriety. "There was a big party thrown by *The Columbus Dispatch* out on a big estate. It was a very exclusive party. Bob Hope was there and I was standing at the bar when General [William] Westmoreland came up. I was talking to the general and he started asking about Woody. He had never met Woody, but had heard all about his visits to Vietnam. I tracked down Woody at the party and introduced the two and they stood around and talked forever. Another time, I was at a grand opening in our student union for a new dining section that included a McDonald's. Ray Kroc, the head of McDonald's, was there to cut the ribbon made out of dollar bills. I was talking to him and he said, 'There's something I'd really like to do, if you can make it possible. I'd like to meet Woody Hayes.' I called Woody's office and he came right over. The two of them went on and on."

Armitage also remembered Hayes had little concern for money. At least as far as his own bank accounts were concerned.

"I got a report from the Big Ten on coaching salaries and it showed Woody next to the bottom in the conference. I called [then athletic director] Ed Weaver and asked him why. He said, 'Woody won't take a raise. He wants any incremental money to go to his assistant coaches.' I said to Ed, 'Give Woody the highest salary in the Big Ten and if he complains, you tell him that we don't want to be embarrassed again by a list like this, and then tell him we'll put his assistants at the top, too, depending on their experience.' We had to force him to take the raise. He was driving around in an old Chevy [El Camino], but that was Woody. He didn't want or need the money."

Chapter Four

The Opponents

Joe Paterno, Lee Corso, Pete Quinn, Barry Switzer, Chalmers Elliott, Jim Grabowski, Len Dawson, Dee Andros, Al Onofrio, Cal Stoll, Jim Mandich, Leroy Keyes, John Ralston, Ahmad Rashad

"With Woody Hayes, what you saw was what you got. He was one of the few people who didn't have a hidden agenda.

—Former Indiana University coach Lee Corso, who today is a commentator for ESPN

I n discussing Woody Hayes, two thoughts move to the fore of Joe Paterno's memory. The celebrated and accomplished legendary coach at Penn State University says Hayes was a great teacher and a man who carried himself without hypocrisy.

"There was nothing artificial about him," Paterno remembers. "I once met him and sat down with him when I was a young coach. He says, 'Let me see your best pass play.' So I draw it up, and he says, 'That's not very good.' That's just the way he was."

The first time Paterno and Hayes met for one of their nail-biting football chess matches, Paterno says he was anxious, but he was also interested in being as obliging as he could with Hayes.

"Before the game we were warming up, and I see Woody heading up the field. So I start walking to meet him," Paterno recalls. "He got as far as the 49. Then he got to the 50, but he would not cross it. He was a very, very unusual man."

Paterno remembers driving from State College, Pennsylvania, to Dallas for an American Football Coaches Association gathering at the old Baker Hotel in 1950.

"We got there around 1:00 in the morning and had to wait for our rooms," Paterno says. "So we're there in the lobby and I notice a group of guys sitting on the floor. And in the middle of it is this guy, a big guy, giving a clinic . . . at 1:00 in the morning. Someone asked, 'Who the hell is that?' And I said, 'Woody Hayes. He's probably going to get the Ohio State job.' The next year, he got it."

The legends meet: Paul "Bear" Bryant jokes in the New Orleans Superdome with Woody Hayes prior to the January 1, 1978, Sugar Bowl in which Bryant's University of Alabama Crimson Tide washed out Ohio State, 35–6. Photo courtesy of Ohio State University Sports Information Department.

Paterno says one couldn't help but be influenced by the things Hayes did or said. "Woody would've been a great teacher," he says. "I always strove to remember and use one thing I'd seen him do. When he was explaining something to his players or coaches, he'd say it one way, then another way. He believed you shouldn't assume everyone learns the same way."

The coach then offers this slice of audio history. "Buddy Tesner [an orthopedic surgeon] played for us," Paterno says. "He asked me to come out to Columbus when he opened his rehabilitation hospital. I did, and at the little ceremony he had a lawyer who once was a manager at Ohio State. The kid used to tape Woody's pregame and halftime speeches. Woody didn't know it.

"So we're there at the ceremony and the kid plays the tape. And you hear [Hayes talking about Paterno]: 'That little son of a "b." Who does he think he is? The smart ass from Brooklyn. Who does he think he is?'" It brought down the house.

Paterno says Hayes was completely committed to his task and that he always came through for his players, "and he could compete. He was tough."

The coach recalls being an assistant at Penn State under Rip Engle, when the Nittany Lions faced the Buckeyes. "We upset Ohio State when they were number two in the nation," Paterno says. "Later, Rip invited Woody up to our place. Woody was magnanimous. There was no bitterness. He said, 'When you play Ohio State you learn something. You fellas beat us. When we saw our undefeated season slip away, we respected you. You beat us fair and square.' He was a proud guy, but he was an honest guy."

* * *

Lee Corso for years was a keen observer of Woody Hayes and the Ohio State program, especially during the time in the seventies when Corso was head coach at Indiana University. "I remember when Woody lost to Indiana in 1951 that he said IU would never beat him again," Corso says.

Well, in 1976 the Buckeyes traveled to Bloomington, Indiana, to play the Hoosiers. Corso, keeping in mind the promise Hayes had made, was determined to capture a slice of history. Ohio State took the lead, 6–0, but Indiana came back to go ahead, 7–6.

"At that point, it had been 25 years since Indiana had beaten, let alone led, Ohio State," Corso says. "So I called a timeout and got the [IU] team under the scoreboard, which read OHIO STATE 6, INDIANA 7. I wanted a picture of it! Woody was so mad that he threw his hat at me. I needed a picture of that! . . . But it looked good up on the scoreboard."

And when the game ended? "Oh, 47–7 don't look too good," Corso says with a chuckle.

The one-time college roommate of Burt Reynolds at Florida State University and current ESPN *GameDay* cohost says he admired

Hayes during the time both were coaches and continues to do so. Corso was a head coach for 17 years at the University of Louisville, Indiana, and at Northern Illinois University, and at Orlando of the now-defunct United States Football League. Throughout his career he says he found himself amazed by the way Hayes comported himself.

"It was the honesty and the integrity," Corso says. "With Woody Hayes, what you saw was what you got. He was one of the few people who didn't have a hidden agenda. Woody was hardworking and he demanded a lot of his players and coaches, but just as much if not more of himself."

When Corso was coaching Louisville, he says Hayes "was very good to me. He'd take me to dinner at the Jai Lai [restaurant in Columbus] and give me a list of the recruits he was not gonna take. One of them turned out to be a guy named Tom Jackson, who had a great career at Louisville and went on to play for the Denver Broncos. There was no competing with him in recruiting. Woody just took what he wanted and left the ones who were too short, too slow, too fat, or not smart enough to get into Ohio State for the rest of us."

Corso and Hayes were known to get into a little football poker now and then.

"Woody coached the offense and left the defense to George Hill," Corso remembers. "I made an oath to myself to get him to walk down the sideline to talk to Hill, but we never could get going enough to make him do that! And another time he comes out of the dressing room and takes his team all the way to the [north] end of the Horseshoe. Took 'em the length of the field. So, I took my team up there, too! He didn't like that."

Corso says the human side of Hayes was something to behold. "He really cared about his players and staff," Corso says. "He would honestly take care of them. He loved his players and coaches."

Corso says Hayes had so many good players year in and year out, but he also had outstanding assistant coaches. "That's why he was successful. And also because of his leadership and the respect he got. But his leadership was like the Bear. When Woody and Bryant walked in somewhere, their presence demanded and got respect.

"The thing about Woody Hayes is that whenever he talked to people, what they were saying seemed like the most important thing in the world to him. He was a great listener. And whatever he said to people, he always kept his word. That's integrity."

* * *

When you played against Ohio State, you really were playing Woody Hayes.

"That's the way it was," says Pete Quinn, the former Purdue University center voted to the Boilermakers' all-time, first 100 years team. "Whenever we were playing another team, we all focused on our assignments, the guys we were playing against. But when we played against Ohio State, we were playing The Legend."

Quinn, who owns a successful commercial real estate business in Indianapolis, says he knew of Hayes even as a youth. "Not to demean all the other great coaches, but to me it was always Woody and Bear Bryant. And Woody was so successful because he was a good judge of talent. He played kids in the right positions. He did intimidate them some, but, hey, they responded."

Quinn, who says he would have his son play for Hayes "in a New York minute" were it possible, played in a 46–0 loss at OSU in 1977 (it was his first start as a freshman) and a payback, 27–16 victory over the Buckeyes at West Lafayette the next season, which was Hayes' last. Quinn remembers admiring the way Hayes ran the team.

"He was team-oriented, no question about it," he says. "But you could see a family quality there. It must have been like playing for your father. Because he was such a known quantity, he was easy to read. For his players, that wasn't so bad; do it the right way and you stay, don't and you're outta here.

"He had so much going for him. He had to be one of the first to be truly organized, and to let his assistants have responsibilities on the field.

"Woody Hayes was a hard-nosed, tough guy one minute, and the next he'd have his arm around you and it meant the world to you. He was a winner and a gentleman."

* * *

Barry Switzer clearly recalled his first introduction to Woody Hayes and the Old Coach never hesitating to speak his mind. Switzer, who later would guide the University of Oklahoma to a victory over Ohio State in an epic battle between two great teams, thought back to being a young assistant coach under Frank Broyles at the University of Arkansas.

"I remember vividly an American Football Coaches Association meeting the first weekend in January in the [sixties]," Switzer said. "Frank Broyles was on the floor making a stand for a proposal for legislation he supported. Then Woody Hayes stepped up—I was sitting behind him—and in a big, booming voice states his opposition to what Frank supported!"

Switzer also recalled being in Washington on behalf of the College Football Association. "Woody Hayes and I and other coaches were staying at, I think, the Washington Hilton. I went down for breakfast by myself to the coffee shop. And I hear this big, booming voice say, 'Coach! Come sit with me.' It was Woody Hayes, and he immediately began to charm me. We began to have a conversation that verified all the things I'd heard. All of a sudden, our conversation led into history. [When the meal was served], I reached over and picked up the salt. Woody Hayes reached over and slapped my hand, and he told me I didn't need the salt, that it was bad for me. I thought, 'My God, this guy is my grandfather!' He always had total control and command."

Of all the classic battles waged in Ohio Stadium, one of the best was the 1977 Oklahoma–Ohio State game. OU entered the game with starting quarterback Thomas Lott suffering from a tender hamstring. "I had not played Thomas Lott. I held him out for this game," said Switzer.

Let it snow, let it snow, let it snow! Until the latter stages of his career, Woody Hayes coached in his trademark short-sleeved white dress shirts. Photo courtesy of Chance Brockway.

Good decision. Lott and soon-to-be Heisman Trophy winner Billy Sims staked the Sooners to a 20–0 lead in the first quarter, taking the wishbone offense right to and through the heart of the OSU defense. It was very close to being 27–0, when running back David Overstreet was called for illegal motion on a play in which he ran the ball to the Ohio State 1-yard line. Switzer said Overstreet had a slight lean before the ball was snapped.

"Right after that, we began the second quarter, and Thomas Lott injures the hamstring. Jay Jimerson, a true freshman, went in for him, and we began fumbling and punting. Then we lost Sims late in the second quarter. Our two greatest players were out. Ohio State got momentum and was coming back."

Indeed, it was a game of catch-up from there. OSU established itself on offense and defense to eventually take a 28–20 lead deep into the fourth quarter. Then, OU's Dean Blevins took over. More of a pure passer than an option quarterback—"He hit some key passes," Switzer said—he drove the Sooners to another touchdown and the chance to tie with a two-point conversion. With nothing but the game to lose, Switzer went for it, but running back Elvis Peacock was stopped short of the goal line. Switzer next called for an onside kick. This time the gamble paid off. The Sooners recovered the ball and another drive was under way. Switzer credited Blevins, and wideout Steve Rhodes, for getting the team into field-goal position with little time left in the game. It was up to Uwe von Schamann.

As the kicker lined up for his 41-yard attempt, Woody Hayes called a timeout. He wanted to ice the kicker, distract him, do anything to make him miss. Something else was going on, though.

"Uwe was out there leading their crowd in 'Block that kick!' He was like a conductor," Switzer said. "I knew the distance wasn't a factor for Uwe. He had the leg. . . . von Schamann hit it right down the middle. It would have gone 66 yards. It cleared the top of the uprights. I said, 'My God, he's gonna kick it out of the stadium!'"

Oklahoma 29, Ohio State 28.

After the game, Switzer tried to make his way to midfield to greet Hayes, who just the night before had made a good impression on the young coach but earlier in the day left him confused.

"The night of the 23rd we were at the Galbreaths' farms. I had a great talk with Woody and he was a great host," Switzer said. "The next morning, he had a glare . . . almost hostile. He had his game face on. Friendships didn't matter [to Hayes] at that point."

And what about that postgame madness, Coach?

"I can see it vividly," Switzer said. "I was hesitant to go out there at first. Woody was coming across the field . . . shoving people out of the way . . . and he didn't see me. Someone from my staff kind of stuck their hand out toward him, and he slapped it away. I never shook his hand. . . . I didn't want to cause a scene with all the media there. Woody was so competitive. His shadow stands taller than anyone's."

* * *

Chalmers "Bump" Elliott was the head football coach at the University of Michigan from 1959 to 1968. He had the utmost respect for Woody Hayes, the football coach.

"He was a great coach, a great coach," he said.

But he didn't really know Woody, the man. "He was a bit of a loner. He didn't hang around too many of the other coaches. He pretty much did his own thing."

The pair's teams squared off against each other 10 times. Ohio State won seven of those games. "Woody's teams were always bigger and stronger than everybody else's. They were a short-yardage team that liked to power you. We had some good days and some bad days, but the one game that stands out in my mind was 1964. We won, 10–0, in Columbus to win the Big Ten championship. That was especially nice since we started eight players on offense from the state of Ohio and another seven started on defense. Woody never said anything about that, but I'm sure it must have bothered him somewhat."

* * *

Jim Grabowski was a first-team All-America running back from the University of Illinois. He finished his college career with a school-record 2,878 yards rushing. He played six years in the National Football League and participated in Super Bowls I and II as a member of the Green Bay Packers. And he was inducted into the GTE Academic All-America Hall of Fame. Pretty heady stuff. So what does "Grabo" remember about his matchups with Woody Hayes' Buckeyes?

"We got our butts kicked!" he says. "My sophomore season [1963], we tied them, 20–20, in Columbus, but they stopped me cold."

Grabowski was held to 11 yards on four carries. With the tie, the Illini advanced to the Rose Bowl and were preseason favorites for the 1964 Big Ten Conference title.

"I was quoted in a newspaper story during the off-season that whenever I felt like slowing down my summer workouts, I thought about Ohio State and that helped me run another lap or push myself a little harder. I found out later that Woody put that clipping on the bulletin board the week of our game and used that as a rallying point for the whole team."

The result? Ohio State beat Illinois, 26–0, and Grabowski was held to 32 yards on 12 carries.

Grabowski kept his mouth shut about Ohio State the following summer. He went on to set an Illinois record with 1,258 yards rushing that season, averaging 140 yards per game. But in the rematch with the Buckeyes, Grabo was held in check again. He had 44 yards on 15 attempts, and Ohio State won, 28–14.

* * *

When Len Dawson, the former quarterback of the Super Bowl–champion Kansas City Chiefs, thinks of Woody Hayes, he says one word immediately comes to mind: recruiting.

"Being from [Alliance] Ohio and being recruited by Woody Hayes was more significant for me than playing against him," says Dawson, who in 1954 quarterbacked Purdue University in a 28–6 loss to Hayes' eventual national-champion Buckeyes at West Lafayette, Indiana. "I knew much more about him [than his teammates did] and that made it very, very special."

Dawson says Hayes' ability to get the lion's share of the great high school football players in Ohio to sign with OSU was not to be underestimated.

"You start with that," Dawson says. "Probably the greatest trait Woody had was to recruit these people to come to Ohio State. I know firsthand how heavily they recruited me."

So how was it that one of Ohio's finest ended up at Purdue?

"They were running the split-T [offense] at Ohio State and had not 'discovered' the forward pass," says Dawson, a prolific high school passer. "I wasn't going to put my health in the hands of some defensive lineman."

Dawson, a Purdue Sports Hall of Fame enshrinee says he remembers Hayes this way:

"To me, as far as Xs and Os, he wasn't the best," he says. "With the talent he had, he could've been better. Three yards and a cloud of dust was the hard way. . . . But I think he was a tremendous teacher. I can't think of anybody who played for him who would say bad things about him. He was the [Vince] Lombardi of college football. He was rough and tough, but he always remembered the guys who played for him."

* * *

Dee Andros was a college football coach for 26 years, the final 11 as the head coach at Oregon State University. He was in awe of Woody Hayes.

"I was very, very fortunate as a young coach at Oklahoma. Woody came down to the university for spring practice," said Andros. "Bud Wilkinson assigned me to look after him. What a guy. It was not only a great honor, but he was just an outstanding guy. I must have heard 100 war stories. And I mean *real* war stories. He had more war stories than anyone."

Andros' Beavers played Ohio State just once: in 1974.

"We were supposed to play Wake Forest. They wanted out of the game because they didn't want to travel all the way across the country to play in Oregon. Me being the good-hearted person I am, I traded Wake Forest on the schedule for Ohio State."

Andros, putting his business savvy ahead of his coaching security, said, "It was good for Wake Forest since they didn't have to travel, and it was pretty good for us since we made three or four hundred thousand dollars. So it was a good trade-off . . . if you don't mind getting the *hell* beat out of you!"

The final score was Ohio State 51, Oregon State 10, but Andros said the outcome was determined even before the opening kickoff. "That stadium seated eighty-eight thousand at the time and, of course, every seat was full. They came running out of that damn dressing room, over 100 strong—at that time we could carry only 60 on the road—and that demoralizes you right there."

Andros asked Hayes for a little payback after Woody retired. "I asked him to come to Oregon [State] to speak at a school banquet. He was here, despite poor health. But that was Woody. He always was a gentleman."

* * *

The University of Missouri football team went to Columbus in 1976 confident, but realistic. As the game was winding down, the Tigers were behind by just seven points and moving the ball.

"We went on a 70-yard march and got close to the goal line," said Al Onofrio, the veteran college coach who was leading Mizzou. "We scored on a pass to get within one point and decided to go for a two-point conversion and the win. The play we wanted to run was from a regular formation with three receivers spread. We were going to roll out and throw to the one that was open. The quarterback rolled out, and two of our receivers were being held by Ohio State's defenders.

"The pass was incomplete, but the officials called holding on one of the linebackers. The thing that made that call a saving factor for us was that in those days we used split crews—half the officials were from the Big Eight Conference and half were from the Big Ten—and a Big Ten official was the one who called the penalty. The ball was moved half the distance to the goal, so we went with an option play and scored."

Missouri held on and beat the Buckeyes, 22–21.

"After the game, Woody was walking across the field with his head down. As I passed by to say, 'Good game,' he mumbled something and kept walking on. Woody had raised a big fuss about the penalty. I still have a picture where he has double forearms up in the air in front of his chest, pleading his case with the officials. The media picked up on it and made a big deal out of it.

"Well, the next day, I got a call at home from Woody. He had watched the films and realized the call had been absolutely right. He felt badly about not giving us our due as we walked off the field. That was his way of congratulating us, even if it was a day later."

* * *

Although Woody Hayes never admitted it publicly, he was upset and angry that Ohio native Rick Upchurch went to the University of Minnesota instead of to Ohio State. Minnesota's coach at the time, Cal Stoll, "heard through the grapevine that Woody thought we cheated to get him. I don't know why Woody felt that way. Rick Upchurch didn't qualify for the Big Ten out of high school because of his grades," Stoll said. "He went to a junior college in Iowa, and our only competition for him was the University of Iowa. All I had to do was convince him there was more to do in Minneapolis than look at all that corn in Iowa.

"Woody was a hero of mine, so I regret that I never got to go eyeball-to-eyeball with him over that. He never did personally confront me."

Stoll was the head coach of the Gophers from 1972 to 1978. Ohio State won all seven games of the series during that time, including the two in which Upchurch played.

Stoll preferred to remember his confrontations with Ohio State while he was an assistant coach at Michigan State University in the sixties. "We had some great teams and got the better of him. There was one year [1965] when he threw the ball, I think, on every down but one in the second half. That was pretty uncharacteristic of Ohio State. Woody's teams were always tough and disciplined. When they were good, they were tough, and when they weren't as good, they were even tougher."

A rare quiet moment for Woody Hayes early on in his career at Ohio State. Photo courtesy of Ohio State University Sports Information Department.

Stoll said the image he'll always have of Woody Hayes is from the annual Big Ten Conference coaches' meetings. "He kind of dominated those sessions. He wasn't always right, but he was never in doubt!"

* * *

"Let me start by saying that I was recruited by Ohio State," said Jim Mandich, a standout tight end at the University of Michigan and with the Miami Dolphins in the sixties and seventies. "My hometown is Solon, Ohio, and my dad owned a saloon there. From my junior year in high school on, I'd be sitting at the bar doing my homework with my dad. Out of the blue, maybe four or five times a year, Woody would be cruising the small rural towns of Ohio and he would stop in and say hello. Most of the time he'd be by himself.

"I came to love Woody and love Ohio State. In my senior year [of high school], the recruiting process went on until May. On a trip down there, I was watching film with Woody and four or five of the assistant coaches. One by one, the assistants starting leaving the room until it was just Woody and me and the projector. He kind of startled me by flicking off the projector, turning on the lights and looking me right in the eye. He said, 'Jim, can I count on you coming to Ohio State?' Naturally I was intimidated. I said, 'Yes, you can, Woody, but first I need to go home and talk to my mom and dad about it.'"

Mandich knew he wasn't going to Ohio State and it had nothing to do with Hayes or the school. "I was a pass-catching tight end. I was watching the Ohio State offense and I think the leading receiver was a guy by the name of Billy Anders who may have caught eight or nine passes on the year. I grew up admiring Paul Warfield, and he was a blocking back at Ohio State. So despite all these great things Woody was telling me about playing for the Buckeyes, I knew it was a bunch of smoke. I would go down there and be an outside tackle.

"I had a deep affection for Woody and respected how principled he was. I beat myself up for a long time in my life because I had lied to this guy, but I didn't know any other way of dealing with it. I went back to Solon, Ohio, and picked up the phone and called Michigan and told them I'd like to go to Michigan. They were delighted. I then called Woody and had to say that I changed my mind. He wasn't happy, but he was a gentleman about it."

That made the Michigan–Ohio State rivalry even more special for Mandich. "Things have changed about that game. Most schools have gone to a more national recruiting [effort]. There was a time when I was at Michigan when we had 18 or 19 out of 22 starters who were from the state of Ohio."

Mandich admitted that he was playing against perhaps the greatest teams in Ohio State history from 1967 to 1969. "My junior year, 1968, we had a helluva team and were competing for the Big Ten title. We went down to Columbus and they beat the snot out of us. With less than a minute left in the game, Ohio State had just scored a touchdown and Woody put Jim Otis in to run in a two-point conversion to make it 50–14."

The Wolverines were more than a little upset. The following season, Ohio State was 8–0 and ranked number one in the nation when it journeyed to Ann Arbor, Michigan.

"Our mental approach that year was revenge. They had embarrassed us and rubbed it in. We were plenty angry and had a new coach, Bo Schembechler. We had improved all season, but still were 17-point underdogs. We beat the hell out of them. The score was 24–12, but we dominated them from the start to the finish."

Mandich went on to star in the National Football League for eight years with the Miami Dolphins, but he still relished that victory.

"Woody never forgave Bo for beating him like that on that day. It hurt him deeply, because later Woody said that might have been the greatest team he had at Ohio State. We beat him badly . . . and I always got *great* satisfaction out of that."

* * *

Ohio State and Woody Hayes had reputations that were second to none, said former Purdue University running back Leroy Keyes.

"We beat them, 41–6, in 1967, and we had a good team that season," Keyes remembered. "Woody Hayes said after that game [played at Columbus], 'That will never happen again. We'll be ready for them next time.'"

Hayes was correct, and Keyes was on hand as a senior Heisman Trophy candidate when he and the top-ranked Boilermakers came calling in 1968. It was the third game of OSU's undefeated, national championship season. In the end, the Boilermaker Express was derailed, 13–0, in a game many still consider to be one of the most electrifying ever to be played in Ohio Stadium. On a sun-splashed Saturday afternoon, the Buckeyes took the field with a purpose. Keyes said before he and his teammates knew it, the Heisman and number one ranking were gone. Ted Provost picked off a Purdue pass and ran it back 35 yards for a touchdown, and backup quarterback Billy Long ran one in to seal the Boilermakers' fate. Bye, bye number one.

"I remember looking over and seeing coach Hayes," said Keyes. "He was almost docile. Oh, he would work the officials . . . but he would wait to see what you could do first, then let his offense dictate things. Their power and their strength took over in the fourth quarter."

Keyes saw Hayes as a taskmaster. "He gave no quarters to anyone. I knew he had them practicing for us the whole year. They were so well prepared, and they knew our favored plays. It brought us back to reality.

"Coach Hayes had character and flair. When he walked in the streets, you knew who he was; he had presence. His players talked about him with such reverence, and if you ever heard him speak you were in awe. He was the Vince Lombardi of college football. You can't say enough about how his players behaved and executed.

"He was a great humanitarian. He stood for trust, honesty, and integrity. It really was a pleasure playing against a Woody Hayes–coached team, but I know this: I can go to my grave and they can put upon my tombstone, 'Leroy Keyes was one-and-one against the Buckeyes!'"

* * *

John Ralston treasured his long association with Woody Hayes. Their teams faced each other just once—in the 1971 Rose Bowl. Ralston's Stanford University team beat Hayes' Ohio State squad, 27–17. But the two coaches squared off numerous times in annual all-star games.

"Those were always interesting games," said Ralston. "One year in Buffalo at the All-America Game, Jack Mollenkopf of Purdue was on

Something's tickling Penn State University coach Joe Paterno and Woody Hayes prior to the kickoff of Penn State's 17–9 loss to Ohio State at Columbus in 1975.
Photo courtesy of Ohio State University Sports Information Department.

the staff with me and Woody was coaching the other team. Jack accused Woody of having Anne [Hayes] scout our practices so he could get an edge. It was only an all-star game, but what a time we had."

Ralston met Hayes for the first time at an annual coaches gathering. "At a coaches' meeting another time, Woody introduced me to General Douglas MacArthur. That was one of my all-time thrills. Woody was ushering the general around before he was scheduled to speak to our group. There was a private cocktail party beforehand, and Woody tapped me on the shoulder and said, 'John, I'd like you to meet the general.' I turned around and shook the general's hand and was so excited, I really squeezed, and forgot that here was an 88-year-old man. I think I hurt him. I apologized very quickly. Woody was so proud to be escorting him around."

Ralston stayed in touch with Hayes, even after leaving the college ranks and moving to the pros. "When I was coaching the Denver Broncos, Woody would come by himself to our team meetings in the off-season and would want to know about our passing game. He never used any of it, but he always talked about it and wanted to learn more.

"He would come out to get into shape. He would pick out a couple of the Rocky Mountains, drive up to the base of a mountain and go hiking all day. That was his way of getting into shape. I spent a lot of time with him in the summers.

"What a guy. He's up there looking at us, and he's one of those I consider not only a great coach, but a great friend."

* * *

Originally known as Bobby Moore, Ahmad Rashad played at the University of Oregon from 1969 to 1971. The All-American was a first-round pick of the St. Louis Cardinals and also played for the Buffalo Bills and Minnesota Vikings. The All-Pro receiver is currently a popular television announcer.

"I probably saw Woody four or five times at various banquets. He was so charismatic that he hooked everybody in. He gave these great speeches to the point that everybody there was ready to go out and win a football game, and we were just at a banquet.

"He was, simply put, a leader of men. As a kid, when I first met him at one of those banquets, it was an honor. When he did those speeches, he always tried to include the athletes on the dais. Here was one of the greatest coaches of all time recognizing me, and I didn't think he even knew who I was. It made me feel so proud.

"My freshman year [before freshmen were eligible to play on the varsity], we played at Ohio State the year they won the national championship. I was on the scout team all week, and we were all laughing, because the varsity had to go and we didn't. Most of our guys were just hoping to make it back to Eugene without a cast. There was no way we were going to beat Ohio State. It was like a dream come true to go there,

Critics point to his temper, but no one could criticize Woody Hayes for not standing up for his team and his beliefs. Photo courtesy of Ohio State University Sports Information Department.

but it was really like being fed to the lions. It was one of those times when no matter what kind of speech the coach gave, you couldn't beat the other team.

"When Woody Hayes was your coach, you always had an edge, because he was just so dynamic. There will never be another Woody Hayes. He was one of a kind. You can talk about Vince Lombardi, but I don't know who else you put in that category."

Chapter Five
The Media

Doug Looney, Jim Murray, Jimmy Crum, John Bansch,
Art Rogers, Chris Schenkel, Skip Myslenski, George Strode,
Keith Jackson, Gene DeAngelo, Joe Hendrickson, Roy Darner,
Dick Fenlon, Bernie Lincicome, Jack Buck, Gary Bender

*". . . he turned to me and said: 'I am a benevolent
despot, and don't ever doubt it.' And I think he was,
in his own mind and in his own way."*
—ABC-TV college football announcer Keith Jackson

Fear and intimidation. That's how Woody Hayes ruled, said veteran award-winning journalist Doug Looney, who covered college football, among other assignments, for *Sports Illustrated* in the seventies.

"That was his calling card," Looney said. "If he didn't have fear and intimidation, he didn't have anything. And that's OK. I don't say that with a snideness."

Looney said his trips to Columbus or into the Ohio State locker room weren't made without detailed preparation. "It wasn't as if I was immune to that," he said. "I did always feel that I needed to be on top of my game."

Perhaps the perfect illustration of that is from an incident that occurred before the Ohio State–Penn State game in 1976. Said Looney: "I had been down at Ohio State before the game. I always used to go to the visiting team's campus first, then go to the site of the game. In Columbus, I had no luck trying to talk with Hayes. He was having none of it. I was failing. So [at State College] I went out with one of his assistants, George Chaump, for dinner. I was railing against Woody. I mean I really trashed him. I was upset.

"So George says to me, 'Doug, you know on game day Woody is so uptight that he gets up at about 4:30 in the morning and goes for a walk to burn off the nervous energy. Why don't you call him about 4:00 in the morning. He'll even be glad to talk to you then.' I think to myself, I have nothing to lose. I don't have one note in my notebook now."

So Looney set his alarm clock, which thankfully rang, and he got up and dialed Hayes' room. After a few rings, he said, a sleepy voice came on the line, "and I start talking as fast as I can [and he recounted, rapid-fire style]: 'Woody? Doug Looney. I hear you're a little uptight. You wanna go for a walk?' And then he says to me, 'You rotten son of a bitch! Don't ever call me at 4:00 in the morning!' Then he slams the phone down. At that point, I figured I'd lost nothing and was getting ready to go back to bed, and there's a knock on the door. I open it, and there's Woody standing there with a huge smile on his face."

Looney had been had! He slipped on his jeans and had a nice stroll with the coach.

"When you're dealing with a character that's larger than life it's a special case," Looney said of his meetings with Hayes, which he estimates numbered 50. "Schembechler, Hayes, Bryant, Paterno. They're all larger than life. But Woody was a notch above. He was substantially different."

Looney remembered dealing with Hayes "in all seasons. I watched him a lot, and I talked with him a lot. I would walk into his office in Columbus and prepare to listen about George Patton and do battle. We had many conversations, and a lot of our dealings were around [the week of] the Michigan game."

One time, Looney said, Hayes came right out with it: "'Goddamn it, you just don't like me.' And I said, 'I do like you; you're just hard to deal with.' He was so irascible, and he made things so difficult for writers. He used to say things like, 'If and when you talk to my players....'"

One time, keeping in mind the right to free speech, Looney did talk with some players. The next day, he told Hayes about it, too, saying it *was* his right and "last night in Columbus, Ohio, I flat exercised it. . . . Woody always thought I was up to no good when I was up to good."

Looney termed the Ohio State–Michigan series a wonderful confrontation between giants. "And they coached their worst during those

Woody Hayes in a jacket? Later in his Ohio State career he actually took advantage of the availability of outerwear. Photo courtesy of Ohio State University Sports Information Department.

games," Looney recalls. "They would get so uptight. Not only did they perform nervous, so did their players."

So why was the Old Man so accomplished?

"Woody made up his mind early on that he was going to be a successful coach, and he was. Not a lot of us can say that and do that."

* * *

Jim Murray, the late, great, decorated sports columnist for the *Los Angeles Times*, got to know Woody Hayes well, especially when Ohio State made trips west for the Rose Bowl.

"The thing that I remember most about Woody Hayes is we always had kind of an adversarial relationship. I remember when he first came to the Rose Bowl, I went over to the hotel one night where the team was staying and all of a sudden I hear this 'Hup-one-two-three, hup-one-two-three.' I look out and I think there's a regiment of troops going by. It was the Ohio State football team. He marched them back from the field. He was leading them like General Patton.

"I got to know Woody down at Salisbury [North Carolina] at the sportswriters convention. He was really a delightful guy to sit down and have breakfast with. He was a great Civil War buff, and I thought I knew a little bit about the Civil War! But I deferred to Woody, because he knew obscure battles, who ran them, and how they went. So, I really kind of admired the guy, but I wasn't surprised when he did what he did [at the Gator Bowl in 1978].

"I remember the broadcasters of the game did not even allude to it. The whole world saw it, and they didn't even mention it. It was Woody's farewell, I guess. He was a rough, tough guy, but he was a very good football coach. The kids all put out for him. I think he motivated them the same way [Vince] Lombardi did [the Green Bay Packers]. He made them feel that, 'We're part of a group that's beleaguered by the rest of the world. It's us against the world.'

"Of course, he also stressed defense. The offense was like a bunch of guys laying sidewalk. They never had any long runs, but neither did the guys they were playing against."

And speaking of running the football, it clearly was Hayes' favorite form of attack. "I think he was famous for the line, 'When you throw a pass, three things can happen, and two are bad.'"

Murray paused to consider other memories. "One year he didn't come to the Rose Bowl, and they had a protest meeting in Columbus. I wrote a whole column saying, 'God, yeah, I wish Woody came to the Rose Bowl, otherwise who are we going to have here to sock photographers, milk the press, and tell you to get out of here?' He socked Art Rogers [of Murray's paper]; Art was only taking a picture [of first lady Pat Nixon] and he whacked him.

"He used to take his team to a monastery the night before [the Rose Bowl], to keep them away from the distractions—whatever the distractions were at the Huntington Hotel. Might be a party of blue-haired old ladies downstairs.

"But he was colorful. Wayne Woodrow Hayes. Somebody told me he lived in the same house all his life and never asked for a raise."

* * *

Jimmy Crum was the dean of central Ohio sportscasters as the anchor for WCMH-TV, for which he worked for 43 years. And for most of those years, Crum devoted much of his free time to charitable causes. Recreation Unlimited, a camp experience that benefits physically challenged children, was his pet project, but his time and soul went into the Ohio Special Olympics, the Easter Seals, and other causes. All of which spoke to Woody Hayes, the coach's quiet donation of time and money, and paying forward.

"Despite his rough, gruff exterior," Crum said, "Woody had a heart as big as Ohio Stadium. He never wanted people to know it, though. That would have negated the intimidation-and-fear factor. But away from football, he was the warmest, most friendly, and most compassionate guy God ever put on Earth."

As for Hayes' contributions to charitable efforts, Crum said the coach was always there and ready to lend a hand.

151

"I guess if I had an idol . . . it would be Woody Hayes. I tried to pattern a lot of the things I've done after Woody Hayes."

Crum delighted in telling the story of the aftermath of Ohio State's 21–14 victory against the University of Michigan at Ann Arbor in 1975. The Buckeyes had run their regular season record to 11–0 and were bound for the Rose Bowl, where they would play the University of California at Los Angeles. OSU had pasted the Bruins earlier in the season at Los Angeles, 41–20. Hopes for another Hayes-crafted national title were running high, but they eventually ran into a buzz saw of a team coached to a 23–10 victory by Dick Vermeil. Crum's was not a football story.

"As we got off the airplane [from Ann Arbor in Columbus], there was a woman who handed Woody 21 roses," Crum remembers. "I saw it happen and then I never thought any more about it. A few years ago, I was over in Indianapolis visiting the Colts practice, and I had lunch with [former Hayes assistant] George Hill, who was with the Colts. He brought up 1975, and he asked me, 'Jim, did you ever hear the rest of the story?' I said I hadn't, and be began to tell me."

Hill told Crum that after the Buckeyes deplaned, Hayes asked Hill to be a guest on his weekly television show later that night. Hill said he would, and in anticipation he arrived at the television station at 11:00. Hayes wasn't there. The minutes began to race past, ticking closer to the 11:30 air time. At 11:25, Hayes walked into the station with a purpose.

"George tells me when he saw Woody he knew Woody had something on his mind. He got that look in his eye," Crum recalled. "He says to George, 'Remember the roses the woman gave me today at the airport?' Hill said he had. 'Well, I found out who had the roses. I picked them up, and I spent the last three hours at University Hospital. George, there are some little old ladies at University Hospital tonight worrying about whether they're going to live or die, and all we're worried about is a damned football game!'"

It was a fairly typical scene played out probably more times than anyone could begin to imagine. Crum, though, made it a point to bring one more such story to light, with "the other side" of Hayes melded into it.

"I had gone to visit Woody at the Ernie Biggs facility," Crum remembered. "I went into his office and I saw an erector set up on his shelf. I said to him, 'Coach, are you going through a second childhood?' And Woody says, 'There's a boy over at University Hospital who is an Ohio State fan.' Then he jumped up and grabbed me by the lapels of my jacket, looked me in the eye and said, 'If you say one f***king word about this, I'll kick you right in the ass!'"

Crum said he wanted Hayes to be remembered by others "for what he was: a great human being, a great humanitarian, a psychologist, a great coach, and a great teacher."

* * *

The benevolent dictator. That's what sportswriters used to call Woody Hayes, says John Bansch, a former reporter for *The Indianapolis Star*.

"Each year, the Big Ten Skywriters eagerly looked forward to the stop at Ohio State," Bansch says. "Usually, football was discussed briefly. Then Woody began talking politics, the environment, and [baseball immortal] Cy Young, who was from Ohio."

Bansch says Hayes often would challenge the reporters. "If you don't believe me, look it up," he would say. And Hayes also saw to it that others followed his agenda. Consider this from Bansch: "He was the last coach [on the tour] to permit one-on-one interviews with his players. Early in the tour, we would only see players from a distance while they were practicing. He then 'broke down' and brought the starters over for us to see close up. He would introduce the offense and have a story about each player. Hayes would then introduce defensive coordinator George Hill and have him introduce the defensive starters; Woody did not spend much time with the defense."

Hayes would tell anyone who cared to listen that when a team passed the ball, three things could happen "and two of them are bad."

Buckeyes fans, meet your new coach. This was Woody Hayes' portrait for the 1951 season, his first at Ohio State. Photo courtesy of Ohio State University Sports Information Department.

He was far better known at Ohio State for his three-yards-and-a-cloud-of-dust offense.

"During one stop, Hayes worked exclusively on the passing game as we watched practice for about an hour—just to show us he knew throwing the football was an option. The quarterbacks probably passed more that day than they did during the entire regular season. Once, the late Gordon Graham of the [Lafayette, Indiana] *Journal and Courier* awoke after dozing and immediately said, 'Woody, your offense is so old-fashioned. If you were coaching basketball, you would have the "center jump" after each basket.' Hayes, without hesitating, said, 'If this offense was good enough for [Amos Alonzo] Stagg, it's good enough for me.'"

Bansch relates one story about the wrath of Hayes that he wasn't able to experience firsthand. "Just prior to when I started the tour, Woody threw the writers and Big Ten commissioner Bill Reed out of practice. He thought there was too much commotion on the sidelines," Bansch says. "The writers and Reed stared through the gate to the stadium briefly, stunned and shocked at the turn of events. They went to their DC-3 and there was silence during takeoff. Once airborne, the only sound was a few typewriters clacking. The silence, and tension, was broken when one of the scribes inquired, 'Is c**ksucker one word or two?' The next year, Woody had chaise lounges and tables with umbrellas along the sideline for the Skywriters. Lemonade was served."

Bansch notes Hayes' commitment to his country, and it had nothing to do with military service. "Several years prior to the gas shortage during the [Jimmy] Carter reign, Woody forecast the problem," Bansch says. "He urged us to unhook the air-conditioning system in our cars, saying it would save fuel. To do his part, he walked whenever he could and would tell everyone he stopped to chat with it was his way to conserve gasoline."

Among the many other facets of Woody Hayes, Bansch remembers this: "At times a tyrant, Hayes did care about his players. During preseason two-a-days prior to the start of school, he conducted basic English classes at night for the players. He contended they had to be able to read and write well to be successful in college and in life. He was proud of the achievements of his players, both in the classroom and after they were graduated."

* * *

Art Rogers deserved to enjoy his retirement after shooting photographs for the *Los Angeles Times* for more than 50 years. But his peace and quiet were interrupted by occasional calls from journalists to ask about one second of his long and productive life.

"Yep, it was the 1973 Rose Bowl," Rogers said. "It was a case of mistaken identity. Apparently, somebody was badgering Woody on the field while he was huddled with some players. I was photographing Pat Nixon. She had been in the parade and then came to the game. Woody's huddle broke up and *ka-pow*! I was kneeling down and when he walked by me he just reached out, grabbed my camera, and rammed it back in my face. They thought maybe I had a cracked eyeball, but everything turned out fine."

The next day the *Times* sought battery charges against Hayes, as well as an apology from him. "He had a record of 21 or 22 earlier incidents where he had hit people in the press. Those had all been kept quiet. The *Times* pursued it so no one else would get hit, but you saw what happened later. I was told that eventually the editors got some kind of letter from the school, but I never saw it. All the charges were eventually dropped."

Rogers says he never took Hayes' outburst personally. "I figured he just made a mistake. The very next year I covered Woody at the Rose Bowl photo day, and he didn't even recognize me. I walked up and he asked me what I wanted. I told him the shots I wanted and he helped me get a photo of his quarterbacks."

Rogers said Hayes as a man with a split personality. "I covered Woody for a number of years. I found him to be a great public speaker, but when he went out on the football field, he became a man obsessed. He was two totally different people. Something that happened on the football field was totally different from what happened off the field. He would kick things and throw his glasses and not even remember it. He was a tyrant on the field, an absolute tyrant. But off the field, he was a pretty charming guy."

* * *

Chris Schenkel was an announcer on college football game telecasts on ABC for 16 years. He and his partner, Bud Wilkinson, did a number of Ohio State games.

"We were doing a Purdue–Ohio State game in West Lafayette. Bud and I always had the luxury of getting both teams' game plans the day before the game. Woody gave us his game plan, and Bud and I were looking it over at the hotel. About an hour later, there was a knock on the door, and it was Woody. He said, 'You know, it's about supper time and you might just go out and leave that game plan here and somebody is liable to break in and get it, and then they'd know our game plan for tomorrow. If you don't mind, I'll take it back with me now.' That's how intense he was."

Schenkel prefers to recall Hayes as a kind and caring man. "I was taping a video promo with Woody in Columbus for the American Cancer Society. One of the advertising people with us, Joel Liska, had his son, Mike, there. We got through the commercial, and Woody was introduced to Mike and his father. Mike was about 10 years old and a wonderful hockey player, but he had diabetes. Woody invited both of them to join us in his office. He went to his refrigerator and pulled out a loaf of bread and told Mike that he was a diabetic, too. Woody then told Mike that his mother was a diabetic, also, and she still was living. He said she baked a special loaf of bread for him every other day. Woody said, 'I want you to take a loaf of my mother's bread home with you and maybe it'll help inspire you and your mother to do the same thing.' They always talk about Woody being tough and hard, but that's one of the softest, greatest things I've ever seen a head football coach take time to do."

* * *

Skip Myslenski was a young reporter for *Sports Illustrated* when he drew the assignment of going to Columbus. He was to interview Woody Hayes and write a story for *SI*'s College Football Preview.

"Everyone knows how much Woody loved reporters," said Myslenski.

Myslenski added a bit more irritation to Hayes by being "a long-haired hippie type," in the middle of the campus unrest in the spring of 1970. "But he was acting the same towards me as he was the other reporters in the group. I can't remember how it came up, but we started talking about my dad. My dad, at the time, was principal of Lakewood [Ohio] High School, which is in the western suburbs of Cleveland. After Woody heard that, for the next two days he did everything but kiss me on the lips. He invited me to his office and gave me everything I asked for. He was a sweetheart. I had no idea what was going on. I got home and called my dad.

"I mentioned to my dad that Woody was very nice to me. My dad said, 'Oh, he was just up here last week recruiting Pete Cusick [the former standout OSU defensive tackle]. He even ate in the cafeteria with all the students.' I figured Woody thought I'd be an in to him recruiting this kid; I'd tell my dad what a nice guy he was. It would help him get the kid."

* * *

George Strode was a veteran newsman who worked for the Columbus bureau of the Associated Press before joining *The Columbus Dispatch*.

"One year I was covering Ohio State at the Rose Bowl for AP," Strode recalled. "He let the Ohio writers—there were probably four or five of us—into his closed practice at a local junior college."

It had been raining and the Buckeyes practiced indoors the previous day. That didn't work, so Hayes took his team back outside, even in the mud and slop.

"The punter was having a heckuva time because the field was so miserable. Woody blew his whistle and yelled, 'Get out of there, let me show you how to punt!'

"Woody had the center snap the ball to him. Woody lost his balance and fell right into the mud. He got up and looked at us. We knew we couldn't laugh or he would never let any of us back into a practice. He said, 'Put that in your f***ing newspapers!' I guarantee you, it didn't see print anywhere."

* * *

Saturday is the most sacred day in college football. It's game day. Millions sit, stand, cheer, or otherwise carry on, urging their favorite teams to score, win, maim, or kill the opponent.

Woody Hayes was an opponent to many, especially to some members of the media.

But for the electronic media, Friday is *the* day. It's a time for taping, homework, interviews, and strategy planning. In short, it is a critical day, one that requires the cooperation of the head.

Says veteran broadcaster Keith Jackson of Woody Hayes: "He was a true, genuine character about the game. . . ." Photo courtesy of Ohio State University Sports Information Department.

Keith Jackson, the legendary play-by-play voice of college football for ABC-TV Sports, says Fridays in Columbus were a little different from what you would find on other campuses. "Most of our dealings happened with him on Friday afternoons," Jackson says of Hayes. "And he was at his best benevolent-despot posture by then. Oftentimes, it was very difficult on Fridays for us to deal with him."

Jackson says it is nothing out of the ordinary for coaches to be a little uptight come 3:00 on Friday afternoons. "But that's when we normally wanted to talk to him, and that's when we wanted to talk to a player or take pictures for the introduction [of the players]."

Conventional football regulations state there shall be 11 men to a side. Hayes sometimes saw it differently. Especially on those frantic

Fridays, Jackson remembers. "Sometimes, Woody would send out 12, 13, or 14."

A team cannot start that many players on one unit. "That's what we'd tell him, but he wouldn't hear us. And that would normally set in motion a very vigorous discussion of things."

A few times, Jackson and Hayes went belly to belly in debate over how many players would be captured on videotape for the pregame introductions. "He'd simply say, 'Either you take the kids I send out there, or you don't get anybody,' and that would set off a more vigorous sort of discussion."

But it wasn't just Jackson who had to unfairly finagle his way through this massive spider's web to accomplish what he set forth to do. Jackson said Curt Gowdy Jr., himself a decorated television executive and the son of the onetime, longtime voice of everything, also was put to the test by Hayes.

"I believe it was before the [1977] Oklahoma–Ohio State game," Jackson says. "Curt Gowdy Jr., at that time, was a production assistant. Woody was really giving him a hard time, through no fault of Curt's. Curt is simply just doing what he's told to do."

Which makes one think that Hayes would be proud of this loyal network soldier. Not true.

"I intervened, and that set off the most vigorous discussion that Woody and I had with each other," Jackson says. "We sort of got it off to the sidelines so everybody in the world wouldn't see it. Anyway, I was luckier than Charlie Bauman. . . .

"Hell, he's the guy who hit Mike Friedman; I don't know if you ever paid attention, but Mike was the bald-headed man who normally worked the sidelines [for ABC]. He was the first cameraman to carry the first mini-cam. In many, many ways, it's lucky that Mike was totally occupied, because I've got a feeling that Friedman would've whupped his ass. Mike was a tough guy . . . I mean a really tough guy. In a man-to-man contest, Friedman would have won that one, I guarantee you. He was a tough son of a bitch."

As difficult or obstinate as Hayes was during the season, Jackson said the coach's personality was quite the opposite in the off-season. During the off-season, Jackson says Hayes "would sit down and talk your damned leg off. But during the season, and on Friday afternoons, he was a tough guy."

Jackson paid Hayes a preseason visit in Columbus late one summer. He and his production crew came equipped with four rolls of film. In Jackson's terms, "Son, that's a ton."

"Woody and I sat on the bench at one of the recreation fields there in Columbus near Ohio State. He talked forever, and he was still talking when the last frame went through. He was a great talker, but not when we needed him to be."

Talk, talk, talk. Open, honest, challenging, provocative, offensive, and, yes, defensive. Woody Hayes could talk with the best of them.

"One year, we used guest coaches as [broadcast] commentators, and Woody came out—I believe the game was Notre Dame–Southern Cal in the Coliseum—and that was the year he wrote his book," Jackson remembers.

Hayes' book, *You Win with People*, was selling briskly, not only in Columbus but across the country at that time. Ever opportunistic, Hayes saw the opening. "He brought some copies of his book, and he was damned determined to plug his book on national television. And he did. Whenever he felt like it," Jackson says through a deep belly laugh. "The first time I brought him in [on the air], he started talking. And he talked it through the replay, through the next play, through the next replay, and through two commercials before Chuck Howard, the producer, finally said, 'Hey, Woody. Shut up!' He was miffed for a little while, didn't say anything for about 10 minutes, and then he finally got into the flow of things. We gave him a chance to promote his book, and that warmed him up."

In the wake of all the troubles and belly-bumping, Jackson says he misses Hayes. "Oh, sure. He was a character. He was a true, genuine character about the game, in his own way. And the phrase 'benevolent despot' is not mine, it's his. I remember we were sitting around some-time, someplace—maybe at the old All-Star Game in Chicago—and in the late hours of the evening, he turned to me and said: 'I am a benev-olent despot, and don't ever doubt it.' And I think he was, in his own mind and in his own way."

Jackson seemingly enjoyed watching Hayes play out the part of the commanding general. He also was on hand to witness Hayes losing his command. It was the 1978 Gator Bowl, which Ohio State lost to Clemson University and during which Hayes punched Clemson middle guard Charlie Bauman.

Ohio State was driving late in the game, going for the lead, when quarterback Art Schlichter's pass was intercepted by Bauman. In cele-bration or in taunt, Bauman waved the ball at the Ohio State bench. Hayes lost a wheel. He slugged Bauman, and then, apparently, one of his own players, Ken Fritz, who was trying to restrain the incendiary coach.

Jackson and analyst Ara Parseghian said nothing on the air at the time. Later, they were unfairly criticized for their silence, but the tech-nical situation left everything out of their control. And to this day, Jackson considers it an unjust black mark on his distinguished career. It's another example of how Hayes impacted someone's life or liveli-hood. Let Jackson explain.

"Back in those days—presatellite days—we had to use the land lines. We had no network feedback line from New York to Jacksonville. So we could not see a 'net' return; we didn't see what was going out over the network. We also did not have a sideline reporter. Bill Flem-ming, who had been the sideline reporter that season, was left home.

"We were 'blacked out' in Jacksonville, which means we could not have had a feed over from the local station, either, because the Gator Bowl contract at that time blacked out Jacksonville so people wouldn't stay home and watch. So take those three factors and add this to it: that Bob Goodrich was the producer, a young producer at the time, Terry Jastrow was the director . . . he was a young director at the time, Donn Bernstein was in his first year as the public relations guy for college football at ABC Sports. He was green, too.

"The old Gator Bowl had an overhang, which means if you stood up [in the press box], you couldn't see the far sideline from the booth we had. And if you sat down, your side-angle line of sight was such that with the 143 people that Ohio State had on the sideline—that's how many were accredited; I specifically sought that information out—if you sat down, you couldn't see that particular sideline. And if you sat down, you couldn't see over the monitors if they were anywhere near in front of you. So, you simply pushed your monitors off to the side and you only looked at 'em when you felt like it or needed to.

"Keep in mind that a television monitor is only one eye. It is a camera delivering that particular picture. So, I don't pay a helluva lot of attention to the monitor until somebody tells me to or until there's a replay."

Jackson remembers that Goodrich decided to use the lone tape machine for graphics, instead of taping what you saw at home. "That's being taped at 7 West 66th Street in New York City," Jackson says. "So what you people saw at home that night was not taped in Jacksonville, Florida. The only tape ABC Sports had of it was in New York. But they didn't have a damned line to feed it back to Jacksonville so we could see it. And it very clearly says on the videotape, a copy of which I have, you hear me say: 'Let's look at the tape and see what caused the ruckus.'"

Jackson is a seasoned, decorated television journalist. But because of the Gator Bowl limitations, not the least of which were his vantage point and the need to scramble to get off the air by 11:00 to make way for the affiliates and their local newscasts—"If we go past eleven, they bitch their asses off to the network"—Jackson, his spotter Jerry Klein, and the Mutual Radio crew couldn't see what unfolded before a national television audience.

"I see Bauman intercept it, and I call it. Bauman goes to the sideline and disappears into that mass of people on the sideline. "The camera angle that you saw at home was from the corner of the end zone. You could clearly see Hayes hit the guy. But from where I'm sitting, on the 50-yard line, I can't see that."

Now, having seen the videotape, Jackson knows that Hayes was swinging for the fences: at Bauman, perhaps at his own players, even at referee Butch Lambert, who escaped Hayes' punch.

"He coached a year too long," Jackson says.

Jackson took countless varieties of unfair criticism for what was viewed as a noncall in a Hayes-caused dramatic and tense situation. He was accused of glossing over the rhubarb. "I was not covering up for Woody Hayes," Jackson says emphatically.

Only five reporters later contacted Jackson for an explanation.

Awkward?

"One big pain in the ass," Jackson said, adding it remains the toughest moment and memory of his illustrious broadcasting career. "Once burned, once cured," he said. "The deeper the water, the bigger the sharks."

* * *

Gene DeAngelo was the general manager of Columbus television station WBNS from 1971 to 1995.

"I used to have a big Fourth of July party every year," said DeAngelo. "I would invite Woody, and he'd always say he could only come for five minutes, but then he'd be the last one to leave. One year I had Lou ["the Toe"] Groza at the party, and I introduced Woody to him. After saying hello, Woody said, 'Let me ask you something, Lou. You guys were playing the New York Giants in 1954 at Cleveland Stadium. It was the fourth quarter and you had third down and long. You guys ran a slant-tackle play, didn't make it, and you ended up losing the game. Who called that goddamn play?' Lou didn't know what he was talking about. That game was 20 or 25 years before, and Woody remembered every play, even though he had nothing to do with the game. Woody went on and on. 'By God, Paul Brown was a damn good coach, but that was a boneheaded call.' Then he proceeded to diagram plays for Lou for half an hour."

One never knew who among Woody Hayes' vast network of luminaries would show up at a game or at practice. In this case, comedian Bob Hope gets a hug from the Old Coach after Hope dotted the i *in Script Ohio.* Photo courtesy of Chance Brockway.

165

DeAngelo said WBNS had the first coach's show in the nation in 1948, hosted by Ohio State coach Wes Fesler. Hayes inherited the live show in 1951.

"When I took over as GM, I found out Woody was getting paid only $100 a show, probably the same amount he started getting 20 years before. I asked Woody if I could syndicate his show around the state. I could have gotten him three, four, maybe five thousand dollars a show. With 11 or 12 shows, that would have been more than he made from the university for an entire year. He said, 'No. I'm a college professor, and I teach life through football. Money's not important.'

"We didn't syndicate it, but I went ahead and gave him a raise to $1,000 a show, but he ended up giving away more than half of his paychecks. He'd give them to the Boy Scouts or children's groups. I saved the canceled checks in my desk for a number of years to show people how generous Woody was."

Once Woody stopped coaching, the station tried using Hayes as a movie host.

"He was an expert on the military. I went out and bought the movies *Midway*, *Patton*, *Tora! Tora! Tora!*—all the great war movies. The first week, we brought in a lot of grade school kids so Woody could lecture them. We put him in front of a big flag like [in the movie] *Patton*. Then we took him down to Fort Knox [Kentucky] for a show where Patton's bedroom is in a museum. We took him to West Point [New York]. One day I read in the paper that the son of [German General Erwin] Rommel was going to be in town for a conference. I set up a studio in our offices, and the program director came up with a list of questions. Woody discarded the questions, because he already knew everything about Rommel's history. It was a great interview. I think the two of them stayed in contact with each other and talked military tactics."

DeAngelo, whose daughter Beverly is a movie actress, also enlisted Hayes to be the analyst on a local Ohio State–Michigan game telecast.

"The play-by-play announcer was Gary Radnich. On the air, Gary credited Michigan with making a good play. Woody jumped in, 'Hey, what are you talking about those guys for? We're from Ohio State!'

Gary said, 'Coach, we've got to be unbiased here.' Woody, still on the air, said, 'Unbiased, hell. We're Ohio State guys and don't you ever forget it. Let those guys worry about their side of the stripes and we'll worry about our side of the stripes. Now I don't want to hear any more on this broadcast about how good those guys are or I'm out of here!' That ended all that."

* * *

Joe Hendrickson was the sports editor of the *Pasadena* [California] *Star News* for 19 years. Hendrickson saw Woody Hayes' love for his players, as well as the players' affection for Hayes. And he saw Hayes didn't enjoy being with the media.

"Through much of his coaching career, I believe Woody considered sportswriters to be his enemies, pests who unsettled his players," said Hendrickson. "He tried to isolate his athletes from these 'pests' by barring interviews after games, and it wasn't until later in his career that he learned how to live with the scribes and they with him. Woody eventually even assumed blame himself for defeats.

"I liked Hayes, but I never felt comfortable near him. One time in the press room at the Huntington Hotel in Pasadena, I stood belly to belly with him as we exchanged verbal abuse. On other occasions, I enjoyed his friendliness and kind words when he was in that mood. One thing is certain: I'll never forget Woody Hayes. Nobody else was similar to him."

Hendrickson credited Anne Hayes with the best description of Woody. "She said, 'It certainly hasn't been a calm and peaceful marriage. But it is darn interesting. I don't think I would want to be married to anybody else. I have to fight 85 to 100 football players for attention, but that is better than one skinny blonde. I don't get upset when I am at a game and some fan calls him an SOB. Why should I? I've called him that myself. Mellowing isn't the right word for Woody. His basic beliefs were still the same. But style changes, and he gradually learned to accept it. He just changed his approach.'"

Hendrickson covered eight Rose Bowls that featured Ohio State and Hayes. "It was my civic assignment to introduce or interview Hayes at the pre–Rose Bowl game luncheon. Because he often cited military strategy of the great generals like Patton, I thought it would be cute to surprise him by placing a military helmet on his head. He stiffened and pulled his head away to make my task difficult. On another occasion I asked Hayes what he feared most about USC and he replied, 'Not a damn thing.'"

Hendrickson said he's not the only one in Pasadena who still remembers Hayes. "Woody began his Rose Bowl career by beating Jess Hill and USC, 20–7, in 1955. Woody agitated western football followers by claiming that four or five Big Ten teams could have done it just as easily. Hill became furious. Hayes also irritated collegiate musicians, saying, 'Bands shouldn't be allowed on the field at halftime and mussing up the turf.'"

Hendrickson had a load of Hayes tales. "One of the best stories I have heard came out of the 1969 game when a good Ohio State team defeated USC and O. J. Simpson, despite an 80-yard touchdown run by O.J. Following the scoring dash, Hayes grabbed his defensive backfield assistant, Lou Holtz, and barked, 'How come O.J. was permitted to go 80 yards?' Holtz quickly replied, 'Because that's as far as he had to go.'"

Hendrickson said he learned to live with Hayes and actually had warm feelings toward him. "One thing I know for sure: I respected him. So did others on the Rose Bowl Hall of Fame Committee. He was voted in the first year [he became eligible], although other coaches had a better Rose Bowl record. I felt regret when Woody's career ended the way it did. That was one of the moments when Woody failed to control his inner self. He deserved a better fate."

* * *

Roy Damer was the top college beat writer at the *Chicago Tribune* during the sixties and seventies. "After Woody was fired, I was in

Columbus to cover a game, so I went over to see him in his office. He was a grandfather for the first time, and his grandson [Phillip] was a year-and-a-half or so. We were shooting the BS, and I asked him, 'Does your grandson call you Grandpa or does he have a nickname for you?' He chuckled, then said, 'Roy, would you believe they've taught him how to say Woody?' That's a tender moment from a gruff old guy."

Damer was one of the top wordsmiths of his day. He was a master with the written or spoken word and took pride in his abilities.

"One time I was in Columbus the week of an Ohio State–Michigan game. After practice, Woody had a press conference. I asked him a question. Woody corrected my English, or so he thought. I don't remember the exact sentence now, but I knew I was correct. I didn't want to mess around with it then, because if you got him mad, he might walk out of the press conference and then no one would have been happy. The next day Kaye Kessler ran the press conference transcript verbatim in the Columbus newspaper [the late *Citizen-Journal*], including my exchange with Woody. Well, a week later I got a letter from a schoolteacher in Ohio, an 87-year-old lady who taught English for 40-some odd years. She wrote, 'Mr. Damer, you are right, and Woody Hayes was wrong.' That's one letter I wish I had saved."

* * *

Dick Fenlon covered Ohio State football and Woody Hayes for a number of years. First, he covered the team from a distance, working for a newspaper in Louisville. Later he joined the staff of *The Columbus Dispatch*. He saw Hayes cajole, criticize, and cater to the media. But whatever the occasion, Hayes was always good copy, even if you couldn't always use it in a news story, Fenlon, a columnist, said.

"After a game he was standing outside the locker room, surrounded by the media. The media kept getting closer and closer, and somebody had a little tape recorder held right up to Hayes' face. Woody took his hand, put the recorder down, and snapped, 'Put that thing away and start taking notes like a man!'"

Other times you could use everything he said. "One summer I was writing a preview story on the team for a national publication. I was having a tough time getting in touch with him. I only needed a few minutes over the telephone, and finally, I got hold of him. He had no idea what I needed to talk to him about, but that week Sparky Anderson, who was managing the Reds then, had closed his office to the press for a day. Before I could even ask him about the Buckeyes, he started going on and on about what a big pain in the butt the press was. He couldn't see how Sparky could put up with the media or why he'd let the press into the clubhouse before and after every game. I was scribbling as fast as I could, and he finally said, 'What is it you wanted to ask me?' I said, 'Nothing.' He wrote his own page one story for me on something I hadn't even called about."

And Hayes could censure the press simply by refusing to discuss a matter.

"I was up from Louisville one year, the week Ohio State was playing Kentucky. He was interested in talking to me about a situation going on with the UK program, so he invited me up to his office the next day. I was waiting outside his office door when I heard him screaming. I was a little hesitant to knock when I heard him yell, 'Now get out of here and don't come back until I'm ready for you!' The door opened and a young guy came out. We're standing there together for a second, and assuming he was a player, I said, 'Boy, he must be a tough guy to play for.' The young man said, 'Oh, no. He's the best guy in the world.'

"As it turned out, it was during the time when the World Football League was playing, and this guy had left school early to go play in the WFL. His team folded, so he returned to Columbus without a job. Hayes had been on the phone getting him an apartment, getting his utilities turned on, and getting him reenrolled in school. When I finally got in to see Woody, I asked him about the situation, but he wouldn't talk about it. He was like that. Despite his public image, which was well deserved at times, he was always doing favors for people without wanting any credit."

* * *

Bernie Lincicome took a circuitous route to become the lead sports columnist for the *Chicago Tribune* and later the *Rocky Mountain News*.

"I played high school football at a small school in Ohio, Crooksville. I was a quarterback and always thought of myself as a 'Woody Hayes Quarterback,' which meant that my job was to turn either to the right or left and hand the ball off. I always blamed Woody for my lack of development into the next Johnny Unitas."

Lincicome wound up attending Ohio State in the early sixties, but not as a football player. "My sophomore year, the school's faculty committee voted not to let the football team go to the Rose Bowl, despite winning the Big Ten title. The students took that decision very personally. I was part of the general student body that milled around campus, then grew angry and broke a few windows at the Faculty Club. I remember marching down High Street to the Capitol, thinking the governor might have some way of changing the decision. The crowd grew to about ten thousand students and moved to the campus Oval.

"Woody Hayes came to the Oval and got on a makeshift platform with some of his players. He addressed the students and asked them to please stop this silliness, go home, and accept the decision, because—and I remember his words—'no football game is worth the loss of your dignity.' If you leap ahead about 15 years, there's some irony to that statement. We did pretty much break up after that and peace was restored."

Lincicome's writing career blossomed in Florida. He had an occasion to interview Hayes prior to Ohio State's appearance in the Orange Bowl against the University of Colorado in 1977. "He seemed like a reasonable man, but it still didn't change my mind about him. I'd guess for five years in the early seventies I didn't admit to anyone that I had gone to Ohio State, only because I was embarrassed about Woody Hayes. There was a series of incidents where he seemed to be losing control, and I just avoided telling anyone that I went to school there.

"I know there are a lot of Woody Hayes stories about his kindness and his insistence on an education for his players, but I just don't have any. The balance is there, but overall, I don't think he did it the right way. Going back to his speech on the Oval—'no football game is worth the loss of your dignity'—he forgot that."

* * *

Jack Buck is enshrined in halls of fame for baseball, football, and broadcasting. But long before he was doing play-by-play duty for the St. Louis Cardinals or various television networks, Buck was a student at Ohio State. He went from making 75 cents an hour in the vegetable department of the Big Bear grocery store to a dollar an hour pumping gas on High Street. He eventually got a job at the student-run radio station, WOSU. That led to his first full-time position in broadcasting as a sports reporter for WCOL radio.

"When Ohio State was deciding who to hire as its new football coach in 1951," Buck said, "*The Columbus Dispatch* was endorsing Paul Brown of the Cleveland Browns. I didn't think the newspaper should dictate who the school should hire, so I said on the radio that the university, not the newspaper, should make that choice. I didn't know Woody Hayes, but I said on the air that he would be a good candidate."

Buck didn't realize how influential the newspaper was. "Some of the fans didn't like it that I had taken a stand against the newspaper and found out where I lived and threw garbage on my front porch."

Among Buck's duties at WCOL was doing broadcasts of the OSU football games. He remembered Hayes' first season.

"When the football season began, I needed to learn more about his coaching style, so I enrolled in a football class he was teaching. Most of the other students were players on the team. I was sitting in the back of the class when Hayes singled me out one day. 'Who are you?' he demanded. His hard-nosed reputation already had been established, so the players were expecting a tough exchange. I told him who I was

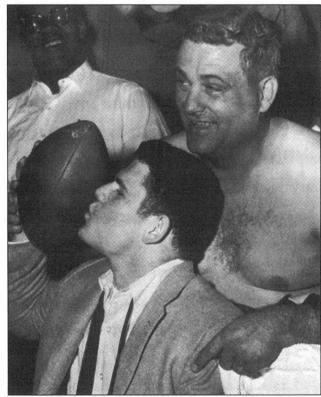

To Woody Hayes and his players, nothing was quite as sweet as a victory, as is evidenced here. During his 28 seasons at Ohio State, the Buckeyes won 205 games. Photo courtesy of Ohio State Sports Information Department.

and explained that I broadcast the games and had enrolled in the class to learn what he was going to try to do. 'Try to do?' he screamed to me. After a moment, he added, 'OK, but don't miss a class. If you miss one class, you're out.'"

A year later Buck was out of the Columbus market, but he never forgot where he got his start and he didn't forget Hayes.

"Years later, when I was doing *Grandstand* for NBC-TV, I was assigned to cover Woody and the Buckeyes during the Rose Bowl. Our cameraman sneaked into the dressing room ahead of time and was filming Woody while he was talking to his players. Woody stopped talking and barked at the cameraman, 'What are you doing?' The cameraman said, 'I'm with Jack Buck.' I walked in about that time and when Woody saw me, he said nicely to the cameraman, 'OK.'"

* * *

Gary Bender was part of hundreds of college football game braod-casts for local stations, as well as national and cable networks. Doing Ohio State games was always a memorable assignment.

"I remember this vividly. I was in Columbus for CBS Radio. I got hold of [then sports information assistant] Steve Snapp, and I asked to go out to practice. Steve had to get it OK'd, and we went. We went out to the old facility and headed out to practice. Here comes Woody, charging at us and screaming. He was yelling, 'Get off this field! Get out of here! You can't come to practice! Who do you think you are?!' It was frightful. I stood my ground, because I didn't know what to do. Steve took off running, but I stayed there. He kept yelling, so I finally got out of there like a scared rabbit. It was one of those deals where your life is flashing before you, some freight train coming at you. Steve and I went back in the building, and all he could say was, 'I thought I'd cleared it.'"

Bender decided to wait. "Like a bulldog, I wasn't going to give up. Lo and behold, he came in and gave me one of the best interviews I've ever had. I don't know whether he was trying to intimidate me or make a scene for the players. I'm not sure what it was, but I'll never forget the two different faces I saw in the course of an hour or so."

Chapter Six

The Friends, Fans, and Foes

Jerry Steinman, Mark Rudner, Alex Gaal, Richard Nixon,

Wayne Duke, John Havlicek, Herm Rohrig, Dave Girves,

John Dewey, Don Canham, Gerald Ford, Dan Devine, Ed Franks,

I. Timothy Tucker, Ron Barry, David Taylor, Colin Gawel,

Rich Randolph, Parker Jarvis

"I guess I expected a personal tirade, but both times
Woody accepted his punishment without a fuss.
I assumed that was the military side of him."
—Former Big Ten commissioner Wayne Duke,
who was forced to issue two official reprimands to Hayes,
both for unsportsmanlike conduct

erry Steinman considered himself "Mr. Buckeye" of the San Francisco area. "I first met Woody when I was in the Zeta Beta Tau fraternity," said Steinman. "He was a Sigma Chi. He used to come to the fraternity once or twice a year and tell us about the benefits of a good education and about paying forward. He would go to any fraternity or sorority that asked."

Steinman, who graduated in 1957, went into the clothing business and settled on the West Coast. In 1974 he was scheduled to undergo the first of five brain operations in Los Angeles. Ohio State was on its way to Pasadena for the Rose Bowl.

"I called [OSU athletic director] Ed Weaver's office the night before I was going to have surgery. They sent me banners and told coach Hayes. Woody didn't really know me then, but he called the hospital every day. When the team got out to California, he came by to see me, even though I couldn't have visitors. Anne came with him, too."

Once Steinman was able to communicate again, he called Hayes to thank him for the support. "That summer I went back to the Midwest. Woody invited my family to meet him at the Jai Lai. I'll never forget that dinner. My brother-in-law was with us and he said, 'Coach, can I ask you a question?' Woody said, 'Sure.' 'Coach, why don't you play Notre Dame?' Woody slammed his fist down so hard on the table, I must have jumped 50 feet. He said, 'Goddamn it!' Then he apologized to the women at the table. 'We don't have to prove anything to them. We're the Big Ten!'"

That was the start of a close friendship. "He became like a second father to me. Whenever he came out to the bay area, I met him at the airport and drove him around. I remember one time we went to the San Francisco 49ers camp. We were in the war room with Bill Walsh and the other front-office people, then went to practice. They let Woody watch from a golf cart. Afterwards, we went to the team dinner and every single player went out of their way to shake Woody's hand and talk with him."

Woody became a frequent visitor, especially when his coaching career ended. "Good friends are hard to find. Woody was the best. He always supported me. Every single day I wish he were still here."

* * *

Mark Rudner was reared in Canton, Ohio. He first was exposed to Big Ten Conference football in 1968 and immediately became a Buckeyes fan.

"I just fell in love with Ohio State football," Rudner, the assistant commissioner of the Big Ten, says. "I went to a game in Ohio Stadium and then couldn't get enough of it. I gradually learned what made up the success and realized that Woody Hayes was a big part of it all. That was the beginning of the legend for me."

Rudner enrolled at Ohio State in 1973. A year later his family, including two younger brothers, were in Columbus for a Buckeyes game.

"Afterwards we went to the Jai Lai for dinner. Woody Hayes was there with several high school prospects. He was seated at a big round table in the center of the room. My 12-year-old brother said he had to go to the bathroom. The next time we saw him, he was with Woody. Woody was introducing my brother to each of the players and signed an autograph.

"Woody could be very charming. He loved kids and used opportunities like that to combat the negative images of him some people had. I think part of the reason Woody was so nice to kids was he was always

Woody Hayes pauses after halftime ceremonies in Ohio Stadium with the framed certificate that signifies his induction into the National Football Foundation's Hall of Fame in 1983. Photo courtesy of Chance Brockway.

recruiting. He planted a seed in each kid's mind: remember me and remember Ohio State."

Following his college graduation, Rudner went to work for the conference office. "I was starting the exact same week Woody was getting out of coaching. But there still were occasions when I had the opportunity to work with him. After Ohio State's [1981] Liberty Bowl appearance I saw Woody in the locker room. He knew I worked for the conference office and he asked me about the health of one of our assistant commissioners. Woody wasn't too well himself, but he was genuinely concerned."

Today Rudner remains neutral in his support of the league's schools, but he'll always have a special feeling for Woody Hayes. "He was, simply, one great American."

* * *

Alex Gaal graduated from Ohio State in 1934. After attending Harvard Business School, he wound up in Southern California. He was named to the Rose Bowl committee and served with that illustrious group for more than 40 years. In addition, he was president of the Big Ten Club of Southern California, a group of one hundred twenty thousand alumni from the league's schools.

"I'm the only Ohio State graduate ever to be elected to the board of directors of the Tournament of Roses," said Gaal. "So it was special the first time Woody came out in 1955. What I remember most about that year is that it rained very, very hard before the game. It was one of the biggest rains we've ever had on New Year's Day. Woody didn't want either of the bands to go on the field before the game or at halftime. He was concerned they might tear up the grass. He was very, very upset, but the committee didn't give in."

Gaal, as an official host to the Ohio State traveling party, had plenty of opportunities to interact with Hayes and his team. "I got very close to Anne Hayes and their son, Steve. The teams used to come out for two weeks to 17 days. You were with these people all day and night, so you really got to know them. What I saw of Woody was not what everyone else saw. He was such a kind person who went out of his way to be nice to people. He was almost like a pussycat. Woody cooperated with the press every day. I saw him go out of his way to help the press a number of times.

"We took his teams to Disneyland, Lawry's [restaurant], Universal Studios, and a number of lunches and dinners. Woody went along most of the time, but I never knew of him canceling a trip for the players, regardless of the circumstances. As we got closer to the game, he sometimes ducked out to do work at the hotel, but he always let his players go and made sure Anne went."

Gaal did see Hayes change his approach in his later years. "For New Year's Eve, he didn't want his team to be around the Huntington Hotel in Pasadena where all the teams stayed. He took his team to a monastery up in the hills, so they would be away from the celebrating crowds. In his later years, though, he relented and let the team stay at the hotel."

* * *

The late former president Richard M. Nixon was a close friend of Woody Hayes. Among other things, Hayes and Nixon joined forces in 1970 at 15th and High Streets on the Ohio State campus in an attempt to quell a campus uprising over the U.S. invasion of Cambodia, specifically, and the Vietnam War in general.

It seemed whenever there was an opportunity, the two would meet—if only for a few hours or minutes. The friendship was cherished by both men. And this is how Nixon remembered Hayes during a eulogy he delivered at a memorial service for the late coach in Columbus on March 17, 1987:

"I vividly recall the first time I met Woody Hayes 30 years ago. It was right after the Ohio State–Iowa football game in 1957. It was a great game. Iowa led, 13–10, in the middle of the fourth quarter. Ohio State had the ball on their own 35-yard line. A big sophomore fullback, Bob

White, carried the ball 11 straight times through the same hole inside left tackle. It was three yards and a cloud of Hawkeyes. He finally scored. Ohio State won, 17–13. It was Woody Hayes' second national championship.

"Afterwards, at a victory reception, John Bricker introduced me to Woody. I wanted to talk about football. Woody wanted to talk about foreign policy. You know Woody . . . we talked about foreign policy.

"For 30 years thereafter, I was privileged to know the real Woody Hayes—the man behind the media myth. Instead of a know-nothing Neanderthal, I found a Renaissance man with a consuming interest in history and a profound understanding of the forces that move the world. Instead of a cold, ruthless, tyrant on the football field, I found a warm-hearted softie *(sic)*—very appropriately born on Valentine's Day—who often spoke of his affection for his boys, as he called them, and for his family.

"I am sure that Woody wouldn't mind if I shared with you a letter he wrote to me shortly after Mrs. Nixon had suffered a stroke 10 years ago.

"'You and I are about the two luckiest men in the world from the standpoint of our marriages, with your Pat and my Anne. I know that you will agree that neither of us could have done better and neither of us deserves to do so well.'

"I saw another Ohio State game on New Year's Day in 1969. The Buckeyes were playing USC, Mrs. Nixon's alma mater, in the Rose Bowl. O. J. Simpson electrified the crowd in the first quarter when he made one of his patented cutbacks after going over left tackle and sprinted 80 yards for a touchdown. But the Buckeyes came roaring back in the second half and crushed the Trojans, 27–16. It was Woody's third national championship.

"He could have quit then, with three national championships and seven Big Ten championships. He had to know that it was a risk to stay on. It is a rule of life that if you take no risks, you will suffer no defeats. But if you take no risks, you will win no victories. Woody did not believe in playing it safe. He played to win.

If you were a Woody Hayes fan, you similarly let your feelings show. Photo courtesy of Ohio State University Sports Information Department.

"In the next nine years, he won some great victories, including a record six straight Big Ten championships from 1972 to 1977. He also suffered some shattering defeats. The incident at the Gator Bowl in 1978 would have destroyed an ordinary man. But Woody was not an ordinary man. Winston Churchill once said: 'Success is never final. Failure is never fatal.' Woody lived by that maxim. He was never satisfied with success; he was never discouraged by failure.

"The last nine years of his life were probably his best. He made scores of inspirational speeches all over the country. He gave all of the honorariums from those speeches to the Woody Hayes Cancer Fund at Ohio State University. He raised tens of thousands of dollars for crippled children in his annual birthday/Valentine's Day phone-a-thons. He gave pregame pep talks to his beloved Ohio State team. He basked in the warm glow of tributes which were showered upon him by those who played under him and others who had come to know him, love him, and respect him.

". . . The National Association of College and High School Coaches capped his career by honoring him with the Amos Alonzo Stagg Award. They honored him as an outstanding coach, but even more important, they honored him as a great humanitarian.

"Two thousand years ago, the poet Sophocles wrote: 'One must wait until the evening to see how splendid the day has been.' We can all be thankful today that in the evening of his life, Woody Hayes could look back and see that the day had, indeed, been splendid."

* * *

The Woody Hayes Persona. That's the way Wayne Duke summed up the Woody Hayes everyone saw and knew. Duke was commissioner of the Big Ten Conference from 1971 to 1989, so he was in position to see lots of the Persona.

"Woody always addressed me as 'Commissioner,' never Wayne," said Duke. "Even after he retired and had an office in the ROTC Building, I would visit him, and he still insisted on calling me 'Commissioner.'"

Despite Hayes' legendary temper, Duke remembered the coach criticizing the officiating to him just once.

"That was actually before I was the full-time commissioner. I was commissioner of the Big Eight Conference and had been chosen to lead the Big Ten just before the start of the football season. It wasn't widely known, but I actually was commissioner of both conferences that one season. I was allowed to keep things going in the Big Eight until a replacement was found, but also got started working with the Big Ten right away.

"I went to Columbus to see Colorado—a Big Eight school—play Ohio State. Obviously, my emotions were mixed. As it turned out, Colorado won, 20–14, but not before there was a controversial call on an onside kick. I was in the Big Eight office on Monday and called the Big

Ten office to check for messages. Woody had called and wanted to talk about the officiating. I called him back immediately. He went on and on about the poor officiating and complained about losing to a Big Eight school. I didn't have the courage to tell him—then or later—that I was talking to him from the Big Eight offices."

Duke cited two examples of how Hayes often kept everyone off-guard. "At one of the Rose Bowls, Woody was accused of shoving [Art Rogers] a photographer from the *Los Angeles Times*. After the game, there was a meeting between Rose Bowl officials, Hugh Hindman, the athletic director at Ohio State, and some others. We decided that until we could get all of the facts, it would be best if no one commented on the situation. Woody was told to keep quiet. About an hour later, I was passing a television and there was Woody, explaining to the reporter exactly what had happened between him and the photographer.

"Then there was the time at the Big Ten Kickoff Luncheon in Chicago. Each coach gets up and talks to the crowd of two thousand or so fans and media. That summer, Michigan State had been investigated for rules violations by the NCAA. It had been rumored that Woody had been the one who turned them in. Well, I'll tell you right now, Woody Hayes had absolutely nothing to do with Michigan State being investigated, absolutely nothing whatsoever. Well, before the luncheon a couple of reporters from East Lansing cornered Woody and asked him about the rumors. He ended up getting into a shouting match in the hallway. I asked him not to say anything about Michigan State during his speech to the crowd. He agreed. But when Woody got up there, he said, 'Yeah, I turned in Michigan State, and I'd do it again!'"

Duke was forced to issue two official reprimands to Hayes, both for unsportsmanlike conduct. "I guess I expected a personal tirade, but both times Woody accepted his punishment without a fuss. I assumed that was the military side of him. You fight and fight, but when an official decision was made, you accept it like a good soldier. That's how he expected the players and coaches he punished to behave, so that's how he behaved."

Duke said he hopes everyone will remember Hayes for his many years of advancing the concept of student-athlete. "He always made sure his players were students and insisted that they all attend classes and abide by all the rules. He instilled a discipline that I'm sure helped many young men succeed in whatever fields they entered. That's what college athletics is about."

* * *

Boston Celtics legend John Havlicek was a member of Ohio State's 1960 National Collegiate Athletic Association championship basketball team. He went on to star in the National Basketball Association and was inducted into the Naismith Basketball Hall of Fame. But did you know that Havlicek almost was a Buckeye football player?

"I was recruited in high school for football more than I was in basketball, and Woody was one of the pursuers," said Havlicek. "I visited Ohio State four times and three of them were for football. Woody was one of the most interesting people that I've ever met. He had a manner about him that was just infectious. He was sincere and the type of guy who grabs your attention. Every word he spoke, you sort of hung on to.

"Woody recruited me heavily and hard. The plan was for me to be the quarterback and Tom Matte to be the running back, which he was initially. When I didn't sign on, they converted Tom to quarterback. I was from a small school [Bridgeport, Ohio] and wanted to play basketball and was going to play baseball, too, which I did. When I told Woody I didn't think I could handle all three sports, he said, 'I want you to come to Ohio State anyhow, because you're the kind of guy we want at Ohio State. I won't ask you again to play football, but if you ever want to change your mind, there'll be a spot for you.' He stuck to his words, but [assistant coach] Bo Schembechler tried to entice me every now and then. I would see Woody in the training room and he would always introduce me as 'the best quarterback in the Big Ten, but he's not playing.' I had people tell me that there was a locker with equipment in it, waiting for me to change my mind."

Havlicek was a physical education major, and Hayes taught one of his classes. "He may have been the top instructor I had at Ohio State. I took his football class, which was a requirement. He was an excellent teacher. He was the type of person who grabbed your attention the entire class period. He was great at telling stories and had great recall. Everyone who took his class really enjoyed it. You could understand his football. He figured you could get three yards and a foot on any play. If you could do that, you'd get a first down. That's how precise he was."

Havlicek clearly remembered one of those displays of recall. "My sister had met Woody when I was a senior in high school at a sports banquet. Four years later when I was completing my career at Ohio State, she happened to run into him at St. John Arena. She was about to tell him who she was when Woody said, 'You're John's sister. I know that.' He even remembered her name."

Always the leader, Woody Hayes stands in during a pep rally in the sixties. Photo courtesy of Ohio State University Sports Information Department.

Havlicek wound up being selected by the Boston Celtics in the first round of the NBA draft, but he also was drafted by the National Football League's Cleveland Browns as a wide receiver. He went to training camp and after four weeks was the final receiver cut.

"I signed my original pro contract with the Browns. My downfall was my inexperience. They needed some depth at that position and couldn't wait for me to gain some experience. But they asked me back six years in a row. I told them, 'The good Lord told me something that first time around.' That was my premonition to stay with basketball. If I had made the team, I was going to try to play both pro football and pro basketball."

* * *

Herm Rohrig held the never-can-win job of Big Ten Conference supervisor of officials from 1968 to 1983.

"I was six-foot-four when I started," Rohrig quipped. "I'm five-nine now."

Rohrig said that despite Woody Hayes' reputation, he complained less about the officiating than most of the other coaches. "Woody was very fair. He was very interested in getting a good officiating job done for him. I remember the first time I went out to the Rose Bowl. Ohio State was playing. Woody took me up to his room with all the films, and he was reciting what he thought the officials ought to be doing. He was really trying to help the program. The only problem with Woody, of course, was that he had a boiling point that would break. That's when he would get into trouble.

"When he did have a gripe, he approached it in a way we wanted him to. He didn't call that often, but when he called, you'd better listen, because he felt he had a real reason for calling."

Rohrig said everyone in the conference office and all the officials respected Hayes. "The officials knew that when he had a gripe, it must be legitimate or he wouldn't be after it. He never said much about officials as individuals, but he would tell me an overall crew might need some work at certain areas. He'd tell me what his thinking was, and we'd go forward from there."

Rohrig said Hayes always had local officials working at the Buckeye practices. "That's why his teams were always down in the number of penalties. If an official made a call in practice, Woody would have the official explain to the kids why the penalty was called. His players understood the rules and the way they were interpreted."

* * *

Mention the Jai Lai to any native of Columbus and among the first recollections of the local restaurant will be Woody Hayes. The Jai Lai opened as a saloon on High Street in 1932 and flourished as a restaurant. It moved to Olentangy River Road in 1955 and remained there until it closed in 1996. It was owned by the Girves family beginning in 1963.

"Woody was there all the time," Dave Girves said. "I'd say he was there two or three times a week. He used to bring recruits and their families. He would entertain other people. He had his weekly press conference there, and he would come by himself. Everyone said it was his favorite restaurant."

Girves recalled two incidents involving Hayes. "He was eating dinner by himself one evening in a booth on the bar side and a kid came up to me and asked, 'Do you think it'll make the coach mad if I interrupt his dinner to ask for an autograph?' I said, 'No, it won't bother him. Go ahead and ask.' Two hours later, he was still sitting there talking to Woody. That's just the kind of guy he was. If you went over to talk to him, he was going to talk your head off.

"Another time, Woody called me on the phone and said his aunt— or some relative—was in the hospital and she loved seafood. He wanted to know if he could pick up a seafood platter to go since she didn't like hospital food. I told him no problem. He came over to pick it up and I told him there would be no charge. He got visibly upset. I said, 'We've never [paid for] your meal in all the years you've been

One of those cold, bitter days in Ann Arbor: Woody Hayes gets his customary police escort off the field in the seventies. Photo courtesy of Ohio State University Sports Information Department.

coming here and I'm not [paying for] your meal here. It's for your aunt and I'm going to [buy] her meal.' He looked me straight in the eye and said, 'If you don't let me pay, I'll never be back.' I knew he meant what he said, so I took the money."

* * *

John Dewey worked in a number of positions at the Big Ten Conference office for more than 30 years before he retired in 1989. He dealt with Hayes many times, and obviously, some occasions stand out.

"Back in 1968," Dewey recalled, "one of Woody's players was accused of selling his [complimentary] football tickets to a known gambler close to Columbus. I went with our off-campus investigator to

Columbus to talk with Woody. It was in the off-season, and we had set up an appointment in Woody's office. He had a very sparse office. It was small and had a metal desk. We walked in, and Woody started lecturing. I don't remember what he lectured on, but it had absolutely nothing to do with our investigation of comp football tickets. He lectured for about 45 minutes or an hour. He just talked and talked and talked. We couldn't get a word in edgewise. After he finished talking, then we talked about what we wanted to talk about. It was amusing to us that Woody was going to control the conversation before we could talk to him."

Dewey remembered Hayes adding excitement to the annual conference meetings. One session saw Hayes square off with University of Iowa coach Forest Evashevski.

"We were out in Iowa City. It was the athletic directors and football coaches meeting together, so there must have been about 25 people sitting around a rectangular table. Woody was sitting at one end and Evy was sitting at the other. Evy was next to [then Michigan athletic director and Evashevski's former coach] Fritz Crisler. Woody accused Evy of cheating. When he didn't get the reaction he expected, Woody got up and walked to the other end of the table, got right in Evy's face, and said, 'You're a cheat. Now, deny it.' Fritz said to Evy, 'Sit down, Evy. Sit down. Sit down.' Evy sat down and let it go. If it hadn't been for Fritz, I don't know what would have happened."

Dewey and the rest of the Big Ten office gave Hayes high marks for his thoughtfulness in 1971. "When Bill Reed, the Big Ten commissioner, died, Woody and Fred Taylor, the basketball coach at Ohio State, were the only two coaches to attend the funeral in suburban Chicago. I'll always remember that."

* * *

Don Canham was the athletic director at the University of Michigan from 1968 to 1988. He was regarded as one of the best in his field, maximizing marketing opportunities as well as revenue. One of his earliest

191

memories of Woody Hayes actually became a moneymaker for Canham himself.

"In 1971, the year Woody tore up the sideline markers," Canham recalled, "I owned the company that made those sideline markers. We used the picture of him tearing up those markers in our advertising. He kidded me about it. I told him I was going to make him famous. We used that picture in our catalog for quite some time."

Canham spent a lot of time with Hayes at Big Ten Conference meetings and social functions.

"I always believed that all great coaches are great actors. They're on stage. Privately, Woody was totally different—at least with me—than he was publicly. You couldn't get him off military history. He was a great military history buff."

When Canham was in search of a new football coach in 1969, he opted for a Hayes disciple. "When I hired [Bo] Schembechler, Dick Larkin was the athletic director down there, and he warned me, 'I don't think I'd hire Schembechler. He's the same as Woody Hayes. You'll end up writing letters back and forth to each other.' I guess one year at the Rose Bowl, Larkin and Woody had a tiff over something, and they weren't speaking, so they wrote notes to each other."

Canham believed that if Hayes were still coaching, he'd be just as successful. "He could coach today. He'd have a different bunch of guys on the field, just like Schembechler would. They'd be the same guys with different behaviors. Those disciplinarians would be as successful today, despite what some people say. Young kids want leadership, and Woody Hayes gave it to them."

* * *

Former president Gerald Ford, who at one time was a standout football player at the University of Michigan, forged a bond with Woody Hayes despite the rivalry between the Wolverines and Buckeyes.

He still considers Hayes "my very good friend."

"Our friendship came about when I was an assistant football coach at Yale, 1935 to 1940, while attending Yale Law School. Woody was

President Gerald Ford and Woody Hayes, Ford's "treasured friend" with whom he first became acquainted in the thirties, talk at a function in Columbus in the eighties. Photo courtesy of Ohio State University Sports Information Department.

beginning his coaching career. We met at various football gatherings. Our friendship expanded after World War II, when I was in Congress and Woody was at Ohio State.

"Woody was one of the most dedicated competitors I ever knew. He was strong, fierce, but always fair. I admired him tremendously because he had great relationships with his players. Woody was most knowledgeable on American political history.

"When I was in the White House he was very supportive. Our friendship continued after leaving the presidency. It was a treasured relationship over many years."

* * *

Dan Devine's teams never played a squad coached by Woody Hayes. If they had, and had switched uniforms at halftime, few fans would have been able to tell the difference.

"We both fundamentally played the same type of football. I wasn't as much of a three-yards-and-a-cloud-of-dust guy as him, but pretty close. There was a group of coaches I met early in my life—Jim Tatum was at Maryland, Bear Bryant at Alabama, Bud Wilkinson at Oklahoma, Bob Devaney at Nebraska, and Woody. We often got together for various clinics or coaches' meetings."

Devine said Hayes was a top clinician, but that group of coaches got a bigger kick out of being around Woody after the lectures were finished. "At dinner, he would talk as if Ohio State University was the only place in the world that mattered. He had a fierce loyalty for the school that bordered on being funny. He wrote a book and took a whole dinner once to explain how hard he had worked to get just the right picture of Ohio Stadium on the cover. He had sent it back time and time again until he got it just right. I was too good of a friend to say anything to Woody at the time, but, quite frankly, I don't think Ohio Stadium is all that good looking. But to him, it was the only stadium in the world."

Despite their friendship, Devine and Hayes didn't always see eye to eye. "[In 1973] when I was at Missouri, we beat Michigan by a pretty good margin early in the season. Ohio State may have tied Michigan for the Big Ten title, but Michigan got to go to the Rose Bowl. I was asked which team I thought was better and I honestly felt Michigan had the better team, so I said so to the media. Well, Woody was pretty mad at me for saying that. But by the time the Coach of the Year banquet rolled around in the spring, he was over it. With Woody, I found him to be very, very unreasonable until you sat down with him and explained your way of thinking. If you explained your position well, he'd be the first to admit he was wrong and wind up agreeing with you. He never got credit for being open to both sides of everything."

* * *

Consider this snapshot from Ed Franks of Columbus:

"In September of 1971, I was one of the squad leaders in the bass section of The Ohio State University Marching Band. We were in the process of grading tryouts.

"To that end, we were all standing in the middle of the band practice field, an asphalt football field immediately west of the stadium. All of the other sections had completed their tryouts and gone in. Our task was somewhat hampered by a driving rainstorm. As we stood there, hands and clipboards taped inside plastic bags, a lone figure came out of the rain. It was Woody, on his way to St. John Arena.

"The coach was all smiles as he shook every hand and exclaimed how much it pleased him to see people 'working out in the rain' and that this was the reason we were The Best Damn Band in the Land. In a few seconds, he was gone, disappearing into the rain, humming 'Across the Field.'"

* * *

Timothy Tucker, the administrative manager for The Ohio State University College of Dentistry, had his brush with Hayes through his father. Said Tucker:

"In 1971, my father, Bill Tucker [age 46], suffered a near-fatal heart attack. He underwent cardiac bypass surgery in 1973. In those early days, such surgery was new and very risky. Also, the treatment of the day included inactivity. As a working middle-class man, my father had to give up his job as a welder at the local paper mill. He had some follow-up complications, all of which led him to a very deep state of depression.

"In 1974, I was working at the university as the manager of the Central Receiving Department. Because we delivered goods to the whole of the university, I became acquainted with the football equipment manager, John Bozick. Knowing my dad's great love for OSU football, I asked Bozick if my dad could get a quick tour of the football locker room. Bozick readily agreed, but warned me that it was the day before the team arrived for fall practice and we had to 'make it quick and not get in the way.'

"My dad was elated over the opportunity to see this inner sanctum. After we arrived, we happened to spy Woody Hayes himself strolling down the hall. My dad was awestruck and was commenting on his

Woody Hayes was always able to get his point across. Photo courtesy of Ohio State University Sports Information Department.

exceptional good fortune at seeing Woody, when it became apparent that Woody was coming straight for us.

"Woody [acting on a tip from Bozick] walked directly up to my dad, and said, 'Are you Bill Tucker?' My dad could hardly respond. Woody instructed my dad to follow him into Hayes' office and told me to stay put.

"After about one-half hour, Woody and my dad returned; Woody said good-bye and quickly disappeared. My dad's feet didn't touch the floor the rest of the day. In that short period of time, Woody talked to my dad about OSU football, the current team, the old days, and, most importantly, life.

"That day with Woody changed my dad's outlook and all but eliminated his depression. Woody did with my father as he had done with so many other people. He took a few minutes of his very precious time and changed the life of a person he didn't know.

"Those of us who have worked at the university during the Woody years knew of his many trips to the hospital to visit friends and people he didn't know. While much of the world only knew and measured Woody as the OSU football coach, many of us in central Ohio were privileged to measure him by his greater humanitarian works. While most of what the rest of the world will remember about Woody Hayes will be printed on paper in terms of scores, statistics, wins, and losses, many of us will remember Woody and his acts of unsolicited kindness in our hearts."

* * *

The Ohio State campus, like most of the nation's schools, was rocked by student demonstrations in the early seventies. Ron Barry was one of those demonstrators in May 1970.

"I and about a thousand 'thrill seekers' were playing hide 'n' seek in the early evening with the state troopers and National Guard near the student union," Barry recalls. "I was a freshman, housed in Lincoln Tower, so I was pretty far from 'home.' Through a slight haze of tear gas, the recognizable figure of Woody Hayes, dressed in sports jacket and tie, emerged from the smoke."

Barry said everyone stopped in his or her tracks. "In the Woody Hayes timbre we know so well, he said, 'Go back to your dorms. . . . Go back to your dorms!' He was only about three feet from me and all I said was, 'Just beat Michigan this year by 50!' He replied, 'We'll do our best. Just go back to your dorms.'"

Barry said about 50 students did just that.

"That was the only time I saw him up close, but I'll never forget it."

* * *

Former Ohio State defensive back Todd Bell was at center stage in Ohio Stadium in 1977. But he wasn't in his Buckeyes uniform. He was still a senior from Middletown High School, competing in the Ohio Boys State High School Track and Field Championships. David Taylor was there.

"Todd had already signed a letter of intent to play football for Woody at OSU," recalls Taylor, a 1981 graduate of Ohio State. "That day he broke the state's oldest and most storied record, Jesse Owens' long jump mark of 24'3¾" that had stood since 1933. Bell jumped 24'6¾" that day.

"My best friend and I were seniors in high school and both ran track. We were down to see the meet and to root on a few friends who we knew and had competed against from other schools. We were also there to see if Bell could do the impossible. We watched the long jump from alongside the track. Suddenly, an elderly gentleman pushed by me on his way out onto the floor of the stadium. It was coach Hayes."

Woody had gone down to the track to congratulate Bell. "When he finished chatting with Bell, coach Hayes turned around to walk up the steps of the west side of the stadium. He was, of course, swarmed for autographs, pictures, and handshakes."

Taylor was one of those fans and cherished the autograph, signed on the cover of his meet program.

"After signing my program, coach Hayes, ever the recruiter, eyed me up and down . . . and asked me if I was a football player, where I was from, what position I played, et cetera. I was more than happy to tell him.

"I was struck at how sincerely he seemed to want to know these things. That is, until I told him I was a kicker. Woody smiled, but immediately, almost imperceptibly, his eyes seemed to glaze over a bit, and before I knew it, he was talking to the kid standing next to me, another big, strapping lad of 18. I guess Woody wasn't recruiting kickers that day."

* * *

Woody Hayes' influence is evident in the strangest places. But a rock 'n' roll band? It's enough to make the ghost of Hayes grab a guitar and smash it to bits on stage, break a microphone stand in two, then lecture the stunned crowd to go home and read a book on World War II.

Colin Gawel was a guitarist/vocalist for the nationally known band Watershed. The three-piece group originated in Columbus and almost named its debut album *Coach Hayes*. Instead it was titled *Three Chords and a Cloud of Dust.*

"It's a Columbus, Ohio, thing," said Gawel. "We're all huge Buckeye fans. We still wear our Woody Hayes Block O hats on stage a lot of times. One time we were performing in Columbus on a Friday night and playing in Wisconsin the next night, so we drove through the night, stopped and saw Ohio State play Northwestern, then played the gig with no sleep. We always play New Year's Eve since it's such a good payday. One year after a gig, we drove straight through to Florida and got there about 5:00 in the morning, got up and went to the Citrus Bowl."

Another indication of the band's fanaticism for OSU can be seen among the group's equipment. "Our bass player has MICHIGAN SUCKS spray-painted across his bass case. No one hates Michigan more than us."

Gawel met Hayes just once. "I was real young, just a kid. They used to practice in the Horseshoe, and at the end of practice, you could just kind of play on the field. I remember Woody just walking around, kind of hanging out. There were a bunch of us kids standing there, and he came over and said hi and shook our hands and asked, 'Are you guys going to be Buckeyes one day?'"

So, would Hayes like and appreciate Watershed's music?

"Ummm, I don't know about that."

* * *

Rich Randolph is a 1969 Ohio State graduate who worked on campus as a computer specialist.

"A young transfer student from New York was hired to tutor a football player," Randolph said. "The tutor didn't have much interest in football and only vaguely knew who Hayes was. He was told to meet the player in a classroom at St. John Arena. When he got there, he was introduced to the player by Esco Sarkkinen, the longtime Woody assistant. Esco asked him to take a seat, saying that Woody wanted to go over some film with the player before the tutoring began. Then Esco took a seat in the back of the room and began reading his newspaper.

"Hayes arrived and introduced himself and then began the film session with the player while the tutor watched. The film was of a Michigan game, played days before, and the game was a loss. Worse yet, the film highlighted many mistakes by the hapless player. When the first mistake was shown, Woody began to hyperventilate. With each successive mistake, he got redder and redder and louder and louder. The player got pale and began to tremble. Finally, unable to stand any more, Hayes picked up a chair and threw it against a wall, breaking it and storming out of the room.

"There were about 60 seconds of stunned silence before Esco looked up from his paper and said, matter-of-factly, 'Oh, you guys can leave now.'"

* * *

Parker Jarvis graduated from Ohio State's dental school in 1975 after a stint in Vietnam delayed his education. He credited a wartime visit by Woody Hayes as making the tough situation bearable, if only for a short time.

"I was at a rather small fire base in Vietnam in 1968 and 1969," Jarvis said. "We didn't get many road shows. Bob Hope would never come and see us. Maybe a Korean quartet was about the only thing that would show up, because it was so remote. I understand that when Woody went over, he wanted to see the people that were in the thick of it, in the boonies. We were really surprised when he came. There was no advance warning. There must have been about 50 of us. Woody showed us football movies on a sheet hung on the side of a bunker. He was as nice as could be and very entertaining."

Woody Hayes: in all the world, there was only one. Photo courtesy of Ohio State University Sports Information Department.

Hayes asked if there were any Buckeyes among the troops. "I don't think he expected any. This was a combat, primarily infantry, unit. You get a lot of high school graduates, but that was about it. I raised my hand. I hadn't graduated yet, but I had been to Ohio State for two or three quarters. When he was done with the movies, he asked, 'Where's that Buckeye?' He came walking up and got within six inches of my face and looked me in the eye. He asked how I was being treated, whether or not we were getting enough food, and if we had dry socks. As soon as he said 'dry socks,' I knew he knew about soldiering. That's the one thing we never had, because it was monsoon season. Every question was out of concern for the soldiers."

Hayes was there with three or four Buckeye assistant coaches, said Jarvis. "He asked me about my mom and dad and asked for their names. The assistant coaches were writing it all down. Then he asked about my wife and any teachers I wanted to say hi to. Six weeks later, he had called my wife three or four times and talked to my dad for 45 minutes. He called my mom separately and talked to her and called the professor I had told him about. That was Woody. He never asked for any adoration or recognition. He was a pretty special fellow."

Woody's Years at Ohio State

"…in the evening of this life, Woody Hayes could look back and see that the day had, indeed, been splendid."

—former president Richard M. Nixon

All-Americans

1952
Mike Takacs, guard

1954
Dean Dugger, end
Howard Cassady, running back

1955
Jim Parker, guard
Howard Cassady, running back

1956
Jim Parker, guard

1957
Aurealius Thomas, guard

1958
Jim Houston, end
Jim Marshall, tackle
Robert White, running back

1959
Jim Houston, end

1960
Bob Ferguson, running back

1961
Bob Ferguson, running back

1964
James Davidson, tackle
Dwight Kelley, linebacker
Arnold Chonko, defensive back

1965
Doug Van Horn, tackle
Dwight Kelley, linebacker

1966
Ray Pryor, center

1968
Dave Foley, tackle
Rufus Mayes, tackle

1969

Jim Stillwagon, nose guard
Rex Kern, quarterback
Jim Otis, running back
Ted Provost, defensive back
Jack Tatum, defensive back

1970

Jan White, end
Jim Stillwagon, nose guard
John Brockington, running back
Jack Tatum, defensive back
Mike Sensibaugh, defensive back
Tim Anderson, defensive back

1971

Tom DeLeone, center

1972

John Hicks, tackle
Randy Gradishar, linebacker

1973

Van DeCree, end
John Hicks, tackle
Randy Gradishar, linebacker
Archie Griffin, running back

1974

Van DeCree, end
Kurt Schumacher, tackle
Pete Cusick, tackle
Steve Myers, center
Archie Griffin, running back
Neal Colzie, defensive back
Tom Skladany, punter

1975

Ted Smith, guard
Archie Griffin, running back
Tim Fox, defensive back
Tom Skladany, punter

1976

Bob Brudzinski, linebacker
Chris Ward, tackle
Tom Skladany, punter

1977

Chris Ward, tackle
Aaron Brown, nose guard
Tom Cousineau, linebacker
Ray Griffin, defensive back

1978

Tom Cousineau, linebacker

Appendix B

Academic All-Americans

1952
John Borton, quarterback

1954
Dick Hilinski, tackle

1958
Robert White, fullback

1961
Tom Perdue, end

1965
Bill Ridder, middle guard

1966
Dave Foley, offensive tackle

1967
Dave Foley, offensive tackle

1968
Dave Foley, offensive tackle

1969
Bill Urbanik, defensive tackle

1971
Rick Simon, offensive tackle

1974
Brian Baschnagel, wingback

1975
Brian Baschnagel, wingback

1976
Pete Johnson, fullback
Bill Lukens, offensive guard

1977
Jeff Logan, tailback

Appendix C

All–Big Ten Selections

1951
Vic Janowicz, back

1952
George Jacoby, tackle
James Reichenbach, guard
Tony Curcillo, center
Fred Bruney, back

1953
George Jacoby, tackle

1954
Dean Dugger, end
Dick Hilinski, tackle
Francis Machinsky, tackle
Howard Cassady, back

1955
Howard Cassady, back
Jim Parker, guard
Ken Vargo, center

1956
Jim Parker, guard

1957
Leo Brown, end
Aurealius Thomas, guard
Don Clark, back

1958
Don Clark, back
Jim Houston, end
Jim Marshall, tackle
Robert White, back

1959
Jim Houston, end

1960
Jim Tyrer, tackle
Tom Matte, back
Bob Ferguson, back

1961
Bob Ferguson, back
Mike Ingram, guard

1962
Bill Armstrong, center
Paul Warfield, back

1963
Paul Warfield, back

1964
James Davidson, tackle
Dan Poretta, guard
Bill Spahr, end
Dwight Kelly, linebacker
Tom Bugel, linebacker
Arnold Chonko, back

1965
Dwight Kelly, linebacker
Doug Van Horn, guard
Ray Pryor, center
John Fill, linebacker

1966
Ray Pryor, center
Dick Himes, tackle

1967
Dick Himes, tackle
Billy Anders, end

1968
Dave Foley, tackle
Rufus Mayes, tackle
Jack Tatum, defensive back
Ted Provost, defensive back

1969
Jack Tatum, defensive back
Ted Provost, defensive back
Chuck Hutchison, tackle
Brian Donovan, center
Jim Otis, fullback
Dave Whitfield, defensive end
Mark Debevec, defensive end
Paul Schmidlin, defensive tackle
Jim Stillwagon, middle guard
Doug Adams, linebacker
Mike Sensibaugh, safety

1970
Jack Tatum, defensive back
Mark Debevec, defensive end
Jim Stillwagon, middle guard
Mike Sensibaugh, safety
Dave Cheney, offensive tackle
Phil Strickland, offensive guard
Tom DeLeone, center
John Brockington, running back

1971

Tom DeLeone, center
Rick Simon, tackle
Stan White, linebacker
George Hasenohrl, defensive
   tackle
Randy Gradishar, linebacker

1972

George Hasenohrl, defensive
   tackle
Randy Gradishar, linebacker
Charles Bonica, offensive guard
John Hicks, offensive tackle

1973

Randy Gradishar, linebacker
John Hicks, offensive tackle
Jim Kregel, offensive guard
Vic Koegel, linebacker
Rick Middleton, linebacker
Kurt Schumacher, offensive
   tackle
Van DeCree, defensive end
Pete Cusick, defensive tackle
Neal Colzie, defensive back
Archie Griffin, tailback

1974

Kurt Schumacher, offensive
   tackle
Van DeCree, defensive end
Pete Cusick, defensive tackle
Neal Colzie, defensive back
Archie Griffin, tailback
Steve Myers, center
Steve Luke, defensive back
Doug France, offensive tackle
Dick Mack, offensive guard
Cornelius Greene, quarterback

1975

Archie Griffin, tailback
Cornelius Greene, quarterback
Scott Dannelley, offensive tackle
Ted Smith, offensive guard
Tim Fox, defensive back
Bob Brudzinski, defensive end
Ed Thompson, linebacker
Pete Johnson, fullback
Nick Buonamici, defensive
   tackle
Chris Ward, offensive tackle
Tom Skladany, punter

1976

Bob Brudzinski, defensive end
Nick Buonamici, defensive
 tackle
Chris Ward, offensive tackle
Tom Skladany, punter
Bill Lukens, offensive guard
Aaron Brown, middle guard
Tom Cousineau, linebacker

1977

Chris Ward, offensive tackle
Aaron Brown, middle guard
Tom Cousineau, linebacker
Jimmy Moore, tight end
Rod Gerald, quarterback
Ron Springs, running back
Jeff Logan, running back
Kelton Dansler, defensive end
Ray Griffin, defensive back
Mike Guess, defensive back

1978

Tom Cousineau, linebacker
Kelton Dansler, defensive end
Mike Guess, defensive back
Ken Fritz, offensive guard
Joe Robinson, offensive tackle
Tom Orosz, punter
Vince Skillings, defensive back

Appendix D
Academic All–Big Ten Selections

1953
John Borton, quarterback

1954
John Borton, quarterback
Dick Hilinski, tackle

1955
Fred Kriss, end
Frank Ellwood, quarterback

1956
Frank Ellwood, quarterback

1957
Frank Kremblas, quarterback
Robert White, fullback

1958
Robert White, fullback

1959
Robert White, fullback

1960
Bill Wentz, halfback

1961
Tom Perdue, end

1962
David Katterhenrich, fullback

1964
Arnie Chonko, defensive back

1965
Bill Ridder, guard
Ray Pryor, center

1966

Ray Pryor, center
Mark Stier, linebacker
Tom Portsmouth, safety
Dick Himes, tackle
Dave Foley, offensive tackle

1967

Dick Himes, tackle

1968

Dave Foley, offensive tackle
John Muhlbach, center
Mark Stier, linebacker

1969

Bill Urbanik, defensive tackle
Dave Cheney, offensive tackle

1970

Dave Cheney, offensive tackle
Rex Kern, quarterback
Mike Sensibaugh, safety

1971

Rick Simon, offensive tackle
Rick Seifert, safety

1972

Rick Seifert, safety

1973

Randy Gradishar, linebacker

1974

Brian Baschnagel, wingback
Pat Curto, defensive end
Ken Kuhn, linebacker
Bruce Ruhl, defensive back
Bill Lukens, offensive guard

1975

Brian Baschnagel, wingback
Pat Curto, defensive end
Tim Fox, defensive back
Ken Kuhn, linebacker
Bruce Ruhl, defensive back
Chris Ward, offensive tackle

1976

Pete Johnson, fullback
Bill Lukens, offensive guard

1977

Jeff Logan, running back

1978

Greg Castignola, quarterback

National Football Foundation Hall of Fame Scholarship Winners

1964
Arnold Chonko

1965
Willard Sander

1968
David Foley

1970
Rex Kern

1973
Randy Gradishar

1975
Brian Baschnagel

Most Valuable Players

1951
Vic Janowicz, halfback

1952
Fred Bruney, halfback

1953
George Jacoby, tackle

1954
Howard Cassady, halfback

1955
Howard Cassady, halfback

1956
Jim Parker, guard

1957
Bill Jobko, guard

1958
Jim Houston, end

1959
Jim Houston, end

1960
Tom Matte, halfback

1961
Bob Ferguson, fullback

1962
Bill Armstrong, center

1963
Matt Snell, halfback

1964
Ed Orazen, tackle

1965

Doug Van Horn, tackle

1966

Ray Pryor, center

1967

Dirk Worden, linebacker

1968

Mark Stier, linebacker

1969

Jim Otis, fullback

1970

Jim Stillwagon, middle guard

1971

Tom DeLeone, center

1972

George Hasenohrl, defensive
    tackle

1973

Archie Griffin, tailback

1974

Archie Griffin, tailback

1975

Cornelius Greene, quarterback

1976

Bob Brudzinski, defensive end

1977

David Adkins, linebacker

1978

Tom Cousineau, linebacker

Appendix G

College Football Hall of Fame Enshrinees

Ernie Godfrey, assistant coach, 1929–61

Vic Janowicz, halfback, 1949–51

Doyt Perry, assistant coach, 1951–54

Howard Cassady, halfback, 1952–55

Jim Parker, guard, 1954–56

Aurealius Thomas, guard, 1955–57

Bob Ferguson, fullback, 1959–61

Earle Bruce, assistant coach, 1966–71

Jim Stillwagon, middle guard, 1968–70

Jim Hicks, tackle, 1970, 1972–73

Randy Gradishar, linebacker, 1971–73

Archie Griffin, tailback, 1972–75

Appendix H

First-Round Draft Choices

1956
Howard Cassady, Detroit (NFL)

1957
Jim Parker, Baltimore (NFL)

1959
Don Clark, Chicago (NFL)

1960
Jim Houston, Cleveland (NFL),
   Houston (AFL)
Birtho Arnold, Buffalo (AFL)
Robert White, Houston (AFL)

1961
Tom Matte, Baltimore (NFL)

1962
Bob Ferguson, Pittsburgh (NFL),
   San Diego (AFL)

1963
Bob Vogel, Baltimore (NFL)
Daryl Sanders, Detroit (NFL)

1964
Paul Warfield, Cleveland (NFL)
Matt Snell, New York Jets (AFL)

1965
James Davidson, Buffalo (AFL)

1969
Rufus Mayes, Chicago (NFL)
Dave Foley, New York Jets (AFL)

1971
John Brockington, Green Bay
   (NFL)
Leo Hayden, Minnesota (NFL)
Jack Tatum, Oakland (NFL)
Tim Anderson, San Francisco
   (NFL)

1974

John Hicks, New York Giants
(NFL)
Randy Gradishar, Denver (NFL)
Rick Middleton, New Orleans
(NFL)

1975

Doug France, Los Angeles (NFL)
Kurt Schumacher, New Orleans
(NFL)
Neal Colzie, Oakland (NFL)

1976

Archie Griffin, Cincinnati (NFL)
Tim Fox, New England (NFL)

1977

Bob Brudzinski, Los Angeles
(NFL)

1978

Chris Ward, New York Jets (NFL)

1979

Tom Cousineau, Buffalo (NFL)*

1982

Art Schlichter, Baltimore (NFL)*

* Played for Hayes. Graduated after his
firing

Through the Seasons, Game by Game

1951

Won 4, Lost 3, Tied 2

Fifth in Big Ten

* OSU 7, Southern Methodist 0
* Michigan State 24, OSU 20

OSU 6, Wisconsin 6

* Indiana 32, OSU 10
* OSU 47, Iowa 21
* OSU 3, Northwestern 0

OSU 16, Pittsburgh 14

* OSU 0, Illinois 0

Michigan 7, OSU 0

1952

Won 6, Lost 3

Third in Big Ten

* OSU 33, Indiana 13
* Purdue 21, OSU 14
* OSU 23, Wisconsin 14

* OSU 35, Washington State 7

Iowa 8, OSU 0

OSU 24, Northwestern 21

* Pittsburgh 21, OSU 14

OSU 27, Illinois 7

* OSU 27, Michigan 7

1953

Won 6, Lost 3

Fourth in Big Ten

* OSU 36, Indiana 12

OSU 33, California 19

* Illinois 41, OSU 20

OSU 12, Pennsylvania 6

OSU 20, Wisconsin 19

* OSU 27, Northwestern 13
* Michigan State 28, OSU 13
* OSU 21, Purdue 6

Michigan 20, OSU 0

*Home games

1954

Won 10, Lost 0
Big Ten and national champions
* OSU 28, Indiana 0
* OSU 21, California 13
* OSU 40, Illinois 7
* OSU 20, Iowa 14
* OSU 31, Wisconsin 14
OSU 14, Northwestern 7
* OSU 26, Pittsburgh 0
OSU 28, Purdue 6
* OSU 21, Michigan 7
Rose Bowl: OSU 20, Southern
    Cal 7

1955

Won 7, Lost 2
Big Ten champions
* OSU 28, Nebraska, 20
Stanford 6, OSU 0
* OSU 27, Illinois 12
* Duke 20, OSU 14
OSU 26, Wisconsin 16
* OSU 49, Northwestern 0
* OSU 20, Indiana 13
* OSU 20, Iowa 10
OSU 17, Michigan 0

1956

Won 6, Lost 3
Tied for fourth in Big Ten
* OSU 34, Nebraska 7
* OSU 32, Stanford 20
OSU 26, Illinois 6

* Penn State 7, OSU 6
* OSU 21, Wisconsin 0
OSU 6, Northwestern 2
* OSU 35, Indiana 14
Iowa 6, OSU 0
* Michigan 19, OSU 0

1957

Won 9, Lost 1
Big Ten and national champions
* Texas Christian 18, OSU 14
OSU 35, Washington 7
* OSU 21, Illinois 7
* OSU 56, Indiana 0
OSU 16, Wisconsin 13
* OSU 47, Northwestern 6
* OSU 20, Purdue 7
* OSU 17, Iowa 13
OSU 31, Michigan 14
Rose Bowl: OSU 10, Oregon 7

1958

Won 6, Lost 1, Tied 2
Third in Big Ten
* OSU 23, Southern Methodist 20
* OSU 12, Washington 7
OSU 19, Illinois 13
* OSU 49, Indiana 8
* OSU 7, Wisconsin 7
Northwestern 21, OSU 0
* OSU 14, Purdue 14
OSU 38, Iowa 28
* OSU 20, Michigan 14

1959

Won 3, Lost 5, Tied 1
Tied for eighth in Big Ten
* OSU 14, Duke 13
Southern Cal 17, OSU 0
* Illinois 9, OSU 0
* OSU 15, Purdue 0
Wisconsin 12, OSU 3
* OSU 30, Michigan State 24
* OSU 0, Indiana 0
* Iowa 16, OSU 7
Michigan 23, OSU 14

1960

Won 7, Lost 2
Third in Big Ten
* OSU 24, Southern Methodist 0
* OSU 20, Southern Cal 0
OSU 34, Illinois 7
Purdue 24, OSU 21
* OSU 34, Wisconsin 7
OSU 21, Michigan State 10
* OSU 36, Indiana 7
Iowa 35, OSU 12
* OSU 7, Michigan 0

1961

Won 8, Lost 0, Tied 1
Big Ten and (Football Writers)
   national champions
* OSU 7, Texas Christian 7
* OSU 13, UCLA 3
* OSU 44, Illinois 0
OSU 10, Northwestern 0
OSU 30, Wisconsin 21

* OSU 29, Iowa 13
OSU 16, Indiana 7
* OSU 22, Oregon 12
OSU 50, Michigan 20

1962

Won 6, Lost 3
Tied for third in Big Ten
* OSU 41, North Carolina 7
UCLA 9, OSU 7
OSU 51, Illinois 15
* Northwestern 18, OSU 14
* OSU 17, Wisconsin 7
Iowa 28, OSU 14
* OSU 10, Indiana 7
* OSU 26, Oregon 7
* OSU 28, Michigan 0

1963

Won 5, Lost 3, Tied 1
Tied for second in Big Ten
* OSU 17, Texas A&M 0
OSU 21, Indiana 0
* OSU 20, Illinois 20
Southern Cal 32, OSU 3
OSU 13, Wisconsin 10
* OSU 7, Iowa 3
* Penn State 10, OSU 7
* Northwestern 17, OSU 8
OSU 14, Michigan 10

1964

Won 7, Lost 2
Second in Big Ten
* OSU 27, Southern Methodist 8

* OSU 17, Indiana 9
OSU 26, Illinois 0
* OSU 17, Southern Cal 0
* OSU 28, Wisconsin 3
OSU 21, Iowa 19
* Penn State 27, OSU 0
* OSU 10, Northwestern 0
* Michigan 10, OSU 0

1965

Won 7, Lost 2
Second in Big Ten
* North Carolina 14, OSU 3
OSU 23, Washington 14
* OSU 28, Illinois 14
Michigan State 32, OSU 7
OSU 20, Wisconsin 10
* OSU 11, Minnesota 10
* OSU 17, Indiana 10
* OSU 38, Iowa 0
OSU 9, Michigan 7

1966

Won 4, Lost 5
Sixth in Big Ten
* OSU 14, Texas Christian 7
* Washington 38, OSU 22
Illinois 10, OSU 9
* Michigan State 11, OSU 8
* OSU 24, Wisconsin 13
Minnesota 17, OSU 7
* OSU 7, Indiana 0
OSU 14, Iowa 10
* Michigan 17, OSU 3

1967

Won 6, Lost 3
Fourth in Big Ten
* Arizona 14, OSU 7
OSU 30, Oregon 0
* Purdue 41, OSU 6
OSU 6, Northwestern 2
* Illinois 17, OSU 13
OSU 21, Michigan State 7
* OSU 17, Wisconsin 15
* OSU 21, Iowa 10
OSU 24, Michigan 14

1968

Won 10, Lost 0
Big Ten and national champions
* OSU 35, Southern Methodist 14
* OSU 21, Oregon 6
* OSU 13, Purdue 0
* OSU 45, Northwestern 21
OSU 31, Illinois 24
* OSU 25, Michigan State 20
OSU 43, Wisconsin 8
OSU 33, Iowa 27
* OSU 50, Michigan 14
Rose Bowl: OSU 27, Southern
    Cal 16

1969

Won 8, Lost 1
Big Ten cochampions
* OSU 62, Texas Christian 0
OSU 41, Washington 14
* OSU 54, Michigan State 21
OSU 34, Minnesota 7

* OSU 41, Illinois 0
OSU 35, Northwestern 6
* OSU 62, Wisconsin 7
* OSU 42, Purdue 14
Michigan 24, OSU 12

1970

Won 9, Lost 1
Big Ten and national (National
    Football Foundation)
    champions
* OSU 56, Texas A&M 13
* OSU 34, Duke 10
OSU 29, Michigan State 0
* OSU 28, Minnesota 8
OSU 48, Illinois 29
* OSU 24, Northwestern 10
OSU 24, Wisconsin 7
OSU 10, Purdue 7
* OSU 20, Michigan 9
Rose Bowl: Stanford 27, OSU 17

1971

Won 6, Lost 4
Tied for third in Big Ten
* OSU 52, Iowa 21
* Colorado 20, OSU 14
* OSU 35, California 3
OSU 24, Illinois 10
OSU 27, Indiana 7
* OSU 31, Wisconsin 6
OSU 14, Minnesota 12
* Michigan State 17, OSU 10
* Northwestern 14, OSU 10
Michigan 10, OSU 7

1972

Won 9, Lost 2
Big Ten cochampions
* OSU 21, Iowa 0
* OSU 29, North Carolina 14
OSU 35, California 18
* OSU 26, Illinois 7
* OSU 44, Indiana 7
OSU 28, Wisconsin 20
* OSU 27, Minnesota 19
Michigan State 19, OSU 12
OSU 27, Northwestern 14
* OSU 14, Michigan 11
Rose Bowl: Southern Cal 42,
    OSU 17

1973

Won 10, Lost 0, Tied 1
Big Ten cochampions
* OSU 56, Minnesota 7
* OSU 37, Texas Christian 3
* OSU 27, Washington State 3
OSU 24, Wisconsin 0
OSU 37, Indiana 7
* OSU 60, Northwestern 0
OSU 30, Illinois 0
* OSU 35, Michigan State 0
* OSU 55, Iowa 13
OSU 10, Michigan 10
Rose Bowl: OSU 42, Southern
    Cal 21

1974

Won 10, Lost 2
Big Ten cochampions
OSU 34, Minnesota 19
* OSU 51, Oregon State 10
* OSU 28, Southern Methodist 9
OSU 42, Washington State 7
* OSU 52, Wisconsin 7
* OSU 49, Indiana 9
OSU 55, Northwestern 7
* OSU 49, Illinois 7
Michigan State 16, OSU 13
OSU 35, Iowa 10
* OSU 12, Michigan 10
Rose Bowl: Southern Cal 18,
    OSU 17

1975

Won 11, Lost 1
Big Ten champions
OSU 21, Michigan State 0
* OSU 17, Penn State 9
* OSU 32, North Carolina 7
OSU 41, UCLA 20
* OSU 49, Iowa 0
* OSU 56, Wisconsin 0
OSU 35, Purdue 6
* OSU 24, Indiana 14
OSU 40, Illinois 3
* OSU 38, Minnesota 6
OSU 21, Michigan 14
Rose Bowl: UCLA 23, OSU 10

1976

Won 9, Lost 2, Tied 1
Big Ten cochampions
* OSU 49, Michigan State 21
OSU 12, Penn State 7
* Missouri 22, OSU 21
* OSU 10, UCLA 10
OSU 34, Iowa 14
OSU 30, Wisconsin 20
* OSU 24, Purdue 3
OSU 47, Indiana 7
* OSU 42, Illinois 10
OSU 9, Minnesota 3
* Michigan 22, OSU 0
Orange Bowl: OSU 27, Colorado
    10

1977

Won 9, Lost 3
Big Ten cochampions
* OSU 10, Miami (Fla.) 0
* OSU 38, Minnesota 7
* Oklahoma 29, OSU 28
OSU 35, Southern Methodist 7
* OSU 46, Purdue 0
OSU 27, Iowa 6
OSU 35, Northwestern 15
* OSU 42, Wisconsin 0
OSU 35, Illinois 0
* OSU 35, Indiana 7
Michigan 14, OSU 6
Sugar Bowl: Alabama 35, OSU 6

1978

Won 7, Lost 4, Tied 1

Fourth in Big Ten

* Penn State 19, OSU 0

OSU 27, Minnesota 10

* OSU 34, Baylor 28

* OSU 35, Southern Methodist 35

Purdue 27, OSU 16

* OSU 31, Iowa 7

* OSU 63, Northwestern 20

OSU 49, Wisconsin 14

* OSU 45, Illinois 7

OSU 21, Indiana 18

* Michigan 14, OSU 3

Gator Bowl: Clemson 17, OSU 15

Index